speaking in tongues

JOSEPH DILLOW

ZONDERVAN
PUBLISHING HOUSE

OF THE ZONDERVAN CORPORATION | GRAND RAPIDS, MICHIGAN 49506

To my wonderful wife

...whose walk with Christ, love for others, and commitment to me have been a shining part of my life. "Her children rise up, and call her blessed; her husband also, and he praiseth her."

SPEAKING IN TONGUES: Seven Crucial Questions
© 1975 by The Zondervan Corporation
Grand Rapids, Michigan

Library of Congress Catalog Number: 74-25334

Printed in the United States of America

Contents

Foreword

When this book first appeared in a private printing, I immediately began to recommend it widely, for I considered it to be one of the most intelligent discussions of tongues I had seen. In actual use the work has withstood the questions of students and provoked the thinking of many. Its preeminent quality is simply that it drives one to the Scriptures — not to some selected passages to prove a viewpoint, but to the whole of biblical revelation on this timely subject.

I am delighted to see this work in a form which will give it wider distribution, for it should now help many more to find their way through the maze of modern confusion on the subject of tongues. There is no doubt that many fine Christians are experiencing something they call tongues, and their experiences are genuine. But as with all experiences, the question is not, are they genuine, but, are they scriptural? Mr. Dillow has clearly set forth the tests by which this all-important question must be answered in regard to tongues.

As a sane and scriptural discussion of this subject, this book must not be ignored.

Charles C. Ryrie

Introduction

It was a typical January day in upstate New York, cold and snowy. I was on my way to visit a couple who had indicated interest in a Christian student movement I was directing at Cornell University. As I drove I prayed, "Lord, make me sensitive to their needs, and if it's Your will, increase their interest in our ministry." Little did I know how God would answer that prayer!

I arrived at their home in the middle of the afternoon. A large German Shepherd barked a few unsettling remarks, and then I was invited inside. What was about to happen that afternoon was the spark that drove me into study and led ultimately to the writing of this book.

They were a lovely and gracious couple in their late fifties, very mature in the Lord — and they spoke in tongues. I discovered that my host was the regional leader of a well-known and quite sizeable charismatic denomination. During my seminary years I had acquired some pretty definite opinions about tongues speaking, as well as a basic scriptural grasp of the issues. This couple made no attempt to bring up the subject, but simply demonstrated interest in me and what I was doing.

Their restraint only increased my curiosity: finally I could stand it no longer, and asked them about the baptism of the Holy Spirit and what it meant in their lives. In a loving and non-pushy way they began to explain how this had had a deep impact for good on their personal walk with the Lord. As I began to suggest scriptural passages that seemed to contradict some of the things they were saying, I realized that I was talking with a very competent biblical scholar. My host was thoroughly acquainted with my viewpoint and ably pointed out the weaknesses in it. He proceeded to nail me to the scriptural wall — lovingly — for the next four hours!

As the conversation wore on into the early evening, it became evident to me that they had no desire to push tongues on anyone, to promote division, to emphasize experience over the Word, or any of the other things you often hear associated with the charismatic movement. Further, in our doctrine of the Holy Spirit I found that we were in ninety percent agreement. But it was that ten percent that bothered me: before talking to this man, I had thought I had all the answers.

As a result of that conversation, I began to go back into the Scriptures to take a new look at my previously held position. I made some important discoveries: many of my initial convictions were strengthened, but, at the same time I developed a new sense of love and personal appreciation for my charismatic brethren in Christ.

One of the tragedies of Christian experience is that many never find a deep and meaningful walk with the Lord Jesus. The charismatic movement has suggested that the answer is to receive the baptism of the Holy Spirit and speak in other tongues. It is this wholesome emphasis on "more" and a "deeper life" that gives me my appreciation for this movement.

Would you like to have a deeper walk with Christ? If it were possible to experience a greater sense of joy of the Lord's presence, wouldn't you be interested? I am!

The question here is whether or not this experience comes through a post-conversion blessing of the Holy Spirit evidenced by speaking in tongues. Before you read this book I ask you to adopt an attitude of considering the possibility that there is no such experience promised to believers in the New Testament. In the pages that follow I will suggest some biblical considerations that I believe will lend support to that idea. If what is happening today within the charismatic movement is not what it is claimed to be, we need to provide a biblical explanation of it. There are some powerful indications in Scripture that the gifts of tongues, prophecy, miracles, knowledge, etc. were temporary gifts, present in the Church only during the first century. To my knowledge, there are no other books in print that attempt to detail the full range of biblical evidence for the temporary nature of the miraculous gifts. Whether or not this evidence is compelling enough to believe, the reader will have to decide for himself.

One final point: in attempting to define the charismatic movement's teaching, generalizations will have to be made. Some within the movement would agree with much of what will be said; many would agree with little of it. It is not my aim to set up a caricature and then tear it down. I will try to present general beliefs that I feel are not supported by the Bible.

All New Testament references are from the New International Version.

1

What is the gift of tongues, and what is its purpose?

Near the turn of the twentieth century, a new religious phenomenon exploded on the American religious scene. As far as we know, this new experience was introduced first through Agnes Ozman on January 1, 1901. She was a student at the Bethel Bible College in Topeka, Kansas. While she is not the first person in modern times to speak in "tongues," she seems to be the first person to have received such an experience as a result of specifically seeking the "baptism in the Holy Spirit" with the expectation of speaking in tongues. From this point on, most Pentecostals have taught that the "baptism of the Holy Spirit" was an experience to be sought after conversion and was evidenced by speaking in tongues.

Since that time, the experience of tongue speaking has crossed all denominational lines until today it can truly be said that Pentecostalism is a third force in Christendom (Catholicism, Protestantism, and Pentecostalism). Its adherents include people from all social strata and ethnic backgrounds. It is truly a universal movement. Many of my close personal friends have spoken in tongues and consider the experience to be a vital part of their worship of God.

Many Christians who struggled for years in futile attempts to experience the abundant life that Jesus offers, mark the day that they spoke in tongues as the beginning of a new and vital experience with God. I know of numerous cases in which lives have been changed, churches revitalized, and even marriages put back together due to personal spiritual revival that was sparked by receiving the "gift of tongues."

The new emphasis in the church on the doctrine of the Holy Spirit has brought a special focus on the gifts of the Holy Spirit described in the New Testament. In all, the New Testament lists twenty-one different gifts of the Holy Spirit: prophesying, serving, teaching, encouraging, contributing, leadership, showing mercy (Rom. 12: 6-8); and in Corinthians the following are added, celibacy (1 Cor. 7:7), wisdom, knowledge, faith, healing, miraculous powers, ability to distinguish between spirits, tongues, interpretation of tongues, administration, apostleship (1 Cor. 12). We add to these evangelism, pastoring (Eph. 4:11), and the gift of public service (Acts 6:2-4). These gifts are special abilities given to the believer for the purpose of building up other believers in the body of Christ. While some of them are clearly supernatural, it appears that sometimes God takes a natural ability and puts it to use in spiritual service. As the title of this book suggests, this book is about one of these twenty-one gifts of the Spirit, the gift of tongues.

I must acknowledge at the outset that the journey on which we are embarking will at times involve heavy thinking and much controversy. It is my sincere desire to treat a rather controversial subject without becoming controversial! For this writer, at least, a man's beliefs about the gifts of the Holy Spirit should not of themselves be a determining factor in the bonds of Christian love.

It is not my desire to contribute to the division that this issue already has generated among many Christians. My focus here will be primarily upon the truth issue, i.e., What does the Bible teach? Ultimately, of course, this statement is reduced down to what I personally feel the Bible teaches as there are some who would not agree with my interpretations. The reader will have to judge for himself whether or not the views presented here are representative of the New Testament writers. I am committed, however, to the proposition that the Bible and not our experiences is the final ground of authority.

This first chapter will deal with a very basic issue, What exactly is tongues speaking? and What is its purpose? Before we can talk about tongues, we have to determine what they are. Are they foreign languages? Languages of angels? Or just unintelligible speech? And why was the gift given in the first place? Is it proof of salvation, or a sign of coming into a closer relationship with God, or maybe a sign of the end times? God must have had a spectacular reason for giving such a spectacular gift.

Let's dig in...

THE NATURE OF THE GIFT OF TONGUES

Many people within the charismatic movement (hereafter called Pentecostals or "charismatics") believe that there are two kinds of tongues mentioned in the New Testament. The tongues experience in Acts 2 is taken to be a foreign language, while the tongues of 1 Corinthians 12 are taken to be ecstatic utterances, or heavenly languages, or languages of angels. In order to deal with this idea, we need to get a glimpse of the background behind tongues speaking in first-century Corinth.

A visit to Corinth

Corinth was an extremely immoral city, full of pagan superstition and idol worship. In the heathen worship there of the goddess Diana the use of gibberish, or unintelligible language, was common. Paul refers to this idol worship in 1 Corinthians 12:2 when he speaks of "dumb idols."

In 1 Corinthians 14:2 and 13:2 Paul refers to "mysteries." This probably is an allusion to the pagan mystery religions prominent in Corinth: in these religions this word referred to the hidden secrets of the gods which only the initiated could know. Those initiated into such mysteries claimed to have contact with the spirit world through emotional excitement, revelations, the working of miracles, and the speaking of unknown words revealed by the spirits.[1]

Speaking in ecstatic speech had an important place in this pagan worship. The words were believed to be revealed by a god or spirit to the priest or devotee while he was in a highly excited or ecstatic state. Through this the worshiper believed that he was having a privileged, intimate contact with his god not possible when he spoke to it in his native language.[2] The meaning of the words was not known by the worshiper but supposedly was known by the god or spirit to whom he was praying.

---

[1] Alex R. Hay, *What's Wrong in the Church, Volume 2 Counterfeit Speaking in Tongues* (Audubon: New Testament Missionary Union, n.d.), p. 31.

For further discussion of the ecstatic speech in the mystery religions at Corinth see Alexander Mackie, *The Gift of Tongues* (New York: George H. Doran Company, 1921), p. 25; and F. Godet, *Commentary on St. Paul's First Epistle to the Corinthians* (2 vols.; Edinburgh: T & T Clark, 1893), vol. II, 174; *Interpreter's Dictionary of the Bible*, ed. Arthur Buttrick (4 vols.; New York: Abingdon Press, 1962), vol. IV, 672.

[2] Ibid.

Kittel mentions the "muttering of words or sounds without interconnection or meaning" as part of the idol worship at Corinth, and notes that it occurred commonly in the cults of various other Greek gods and goddesses as well.[3]

So in 1 Corinthians 14 Paul is dealing with an error that the Corinthians had fallen into regarding the speaking in tongues: they had begun to use it in the same manner as the heathen did. They were bringing over their old use of ecstatic speech from Diana worship and using the legitimate gift of tongues in a similar way.

Paul was concerned about the Corinthians' view of access to God. No gift of the Spirit was given for speaking to God: it was not necessary. Christ did not speak to God through a heavenly language manifested by the Spirit. The gifts of the Spirit were all given for speaking and otherwise ministering to men. That one could communicate better with the gods through a language of the gods was the heathen belief. The believer in Christ knows that he has just to lift his heart to God and God understands him better than he understands himself.

But Paul's main concern was the building up of the body of believers as a whole; this was being hindered by the Corinthians' misuse of tongues. In their heathen days these believers had thought that when they spoke in ecstatic speech or gibberish they were speaking secrets or mysteries with their god. The benefit was received by the worshiper alone; no one else understood. The worshiper profited through the ecstasy of feeling

_____
3 *Theological Dictionary of the New Testament,* ed. Gerhard Kittel (9 vols.; Grand Rapids: Eerdmans, 1967), I, 722. One of the key characteristics of the tongues speech in the mystery religions was the lack of connection with the mental processes. They prayed without the mind being engaged.

aroused and the sense that he was really partici-
pating with the spirits in the inner circle. He had
no thought for the building up of the other wor-
shipers. Paul contrasts this selfish objective with
the Christian objective, admonishing the Corinthians to "try to excel in gifts that build up the
church" (1 Cor. 14:12b).

Superstition — then and now

I would like to draw a parallel between the
Corinthian church and some believers today concerning superstition. The root of superstition is
incomplete knowledge of God. Superstition creeps
into the church of Christ when there is a lack of
knowledge of the Word of God. The dictionary
defines superstition this way:

> A belief or notion entertained, regardless of reason
> or knowledge, of the ominous significance of a par-
> ticular thing, circumstance, occurrence, proceeding,
> or the like.[4]

When the heathen attributed spiritual power
or meaning to ecstatic languages which had no
meaning, that was superstition. Modern-day believers must have their convictions based on sound
biblical truths, or else those convictions must be
classified as non-Christian superstition which has
carried over into their Christian life. Today many
believers' ideas concerning the Holy Spirit are not
based solidly on truth, due to a lack of knowledge of scriptural teachings. So as we look at what
the Bible says about the gift of tongues, let's make
a kind of "superstition check" on our doctrine!
Now back to the Corinthians...

Two kinds of tongues?

As mentioned above, the general view of the
charismatic movement is that there are two kinds

---

[4] *The American College Dictionary*, ed. C. L. Barnhart (New
York: Random House, 1959), p. 1216.

of tongues mentioned in the Bible. In Acts 2 there is a possibility that known languages here on earth are spoken. But 1 Corinthians 12-14 clearly refers to ecstatic utterances. Some Pentecostals and some non-Pentecostals believe that the tongues in 1 Corinthians 12-14 and the ones in Acts 2 are ecstatic gibberish.

It is important to note that the ecstatic utterance view came with the advent of the denial of the supernatural and the higher criticism against the Bible in the eighteenth and nineteenth centuries. The critics attempted to identify the tongues speaking of 1 Corinthians 14 *totally* with the psychological pagan tongue speaking of the mystery religions. Their motivations were to remove the supernatural out of the Bible. This was most certainly behind the translation in the *New English Bible,* "ecstatic utterance" for the Greek word, *glossa,* tongue or language. The translators read their theological and antisupernatural convictions into their translation and didn't let the text speak for itself. It is possible that the word *glossa* could be translated "ecstatic utterance" but that is not its normal use.[5]

With this background in mind, let's examine the passages commonly cited by Pentecostals that there are two kinds of tongues in the New Testament.

Uttering "mysteries"

1 Corinthians 14:2 reads:

> For anyone who speaks in a tongue does not speak to men but to God. Indeed, no one understands him; he utters mysteries with his spirit.

5 Robert H. Gundry, "Ecstatic Utterance (N.E.B.)?" *Journal of Theological Studies,* vol. 17, 1966, pp. 299-307. This is a very thorough analysis of the ecstatic utterance translation of the New English Bible. Dr. Gundry shows that the tongues speech of both Acts 2 and 1 Corinthians 12-14 can refer only to known languages spoken here on earth.

This is taken to indicate that the language referred to is other than earthly, because only God understands it, and no one else does. But this could just as easily be taken to mean that no one understands it because it is not his native tongue. If there are no other speakers of the language present, God is effectually the only One being addressed.

The "mysteries" referred to here refer to that which the Corinthians used to do before they became Christians. Using the legitimate gift of tongues for "speaking intimate personal mysteries" between them and their God just as they used to do in Diana worship was a mistake. The same superstitious belief that this actually was creating a genuine intimacy with their God was being carried over.

Praying in the spirit: holy or human?

> For this reason the man who speaks in a tongue should pray that he may interpret what he says. For if I pray in a tongue, my spirit prays, but my mind is unfruitful. So what shall I do? I will pray with my spirit, but I will also pray with my mind; I will sing with my spirit, but I will also sing with my mind.

From this passage (1 Cor. 14:13-15) it often is concluded that two kinds of tongues are referred to: those connected with the spirit (ecstatic utterances) and those connected with the understanding (known languages). Let's see if this is actually what the text is teaching.

All prayer utilizes the human spirit (*my* spirit, v. 14), so to pray "in the spirit" refers to any prayer, whether one is praying in one's own language or in a tongue. When one prays in a tongue, the human spirit is praying, but Paul says the mind is not involved. So, he says, when one prays he will engage his mind also, that is, he will speak in his native language. The contrast here is not praying "in the spirit" (praying in tongues) versus praying "out of the spirit" (praying in one's native language). Because all prayer is "in the spirit," the contrast that results is between praying in the spirit without understanding (in tongues) versus praying in the spirit with understanding (in one's native language), which Paul says he prefers to do (v. 19) in the church.

The phrase "unknown tongues"

The presence of the italicized word "unknown" in the King James translation of verses 2, 4, 13, 14, and 19 has led some to conclude that this refers to a language not known here on earth. The fact that it is italicized, however, shows that it was not in the Greek text to begin with, so we had better not build a doctrine on it! The New International Version translates the phrase as simply "tongue."

Tongues of angels

In 1 Corinthians 13:1 we read: "If I speak in the tongues of men and of angels...." Some believe that the "tongues of men" refers to known earthly languages, such as were used in Acts 2, while the "tongues of angels" refers to a heavenly language to be used by men for private devotion of prayer and praise.

To make this distinction is to read more into the text than is actually there. Paul probably is using exaggeration to make a point, the point being that it doesn't make any difference what language or tongue you speak if you don't have love. Thus when he speaks of "tongues of angels" he is choosing something that would be hypothetically considered to be even greater than the gift of tongues, namely, the ability of speaking in angelic languages. He doesn't specifically say that such languages exist.

The hypothetical nature of Paul's statements seems to be emphasized by the references to "all" in the following verses. "If I have the gift of prophecy, and can fathom *all* mysteries and *all* knowledge, and if I have a faith that can move mountains..." (1 Cor. 13:2). "If I give *all* I possess to the poor..." (1 Cor. 13:3). Paul is not saying that it is possible to fathom *all* mysteries or to possess *all* knowledge or that he has ever moved a mountain with his faith. Neither is he saying that the tongues of angels actually exist. He is speaking hypothetically. In fact, the Greek construction he uses is known in Greek as a third class condition (*ean* plus the subjunctive), and stresses a hypothetical) "maybe yes, maybe no" kind of condition.

Even if this does refer to actual languages spoken by angels, we cannot conclude that men would be able to speak in these languages, or that the gift of tongues consists of these languages.

What Paul does say is that even if you could speak in this kind of language, it would be valueless if you had no love. So we see that the contrast is not between two existing kinds of tongues, but between the true gift of tongues, speaking in foreign languages, and a hypothetical language that would be even better.

We could accurately paraphrase Paul's thought like this:

> Though I speak with the tongues of men, or even if I could speak with the tongues of angels (not that there is anything such as tongues of angels), it would be valueless if I had no love. So quit overemphasizing a few miraculous gifts and concentrate rather on love.

The need for interpretation in 1 Corinthians

It is sometimes argued that the fact that a gift

of interpretation was required in Corinthians and not at Pentecost (Acts 2), suggests that the tongues in Acts 2 were languages but the tongues in 1 Corinthians were ecstatic utterances. The miraculous nature of the tongues which would produce amazement to a non-believer in Corinth was that the non-believer heard a foreign language he did not understand followed by a miraculous translation back into the native tongue of the non-believer. Without translation, the tongue might appear as meaningless gibberish. The effectiveness of glossolalia as an authenticating sign depended on its *difference* from the ecstatic gobbledegook in Hellenistic religion.[6] On the other hand, the amazement factor on the Day of Pentecost consisted in the recognizing by non-Palestinians of their native languages being spoken by uneducated Galilean peasants and fishermen (Acts 2:7). At Corinth the gift of interpretation was necessary not because the tongues there were ecstatic utterances, but because the audience there spoke only one or two languages (Greek and Latin). At Pentecost, the gift of interpretation was not necessary because the audience was from all over the ancient world and spoke numerous languages (Acts 2:8-11).

The charge of drunkenness in Acts 2:13

Some have argued that the charge of drunkenness suggests that the disciples were speaking in ecstatic utterances. However, we should note that the accusers were other than the non-Palestinians ("Some," *etteroi*, Acts 2:13, others of a different kind, i.e., others than the non-Palestinians mentioned in the preceding context). Thus those making the charge of drunkenness were the Pales-

---

6 Ibid., p. 303.

tinian Jews whom Peter addresses in Acts 2:14. They could not understand the non-Palestinian languages that the disciples were speaking. To the Jew in Palestine this sounded like babble and drunkenness. The non-Palestinian Jews however, did not charge them with drunkenness but instead were amazed and perplexed (Acts 2:12) because they had heard men speaking in their native tongues without having learned them.

I think we're on shaky ground when we argue for two kinds of tongues. But there are solid reasons for believing that all the references to tongues in the New Testament refer to only one kind of tongues. Let's look at the evidence.

Consistent usage of "glossa"

The Greek word *glossa* may be translated "ecstatic utterances";[7] however, its consistent usage in the New Testament in every other instance is as "foreign language."[8] In fact the word *glossa* occurs thirty times in the Greek Old Testament, and in every instance it refers to a known language spoken on earth.[9] So to come to 1 Corinthians 12-14 and suggest that here it means something different from what it means in the rest of the New Testament is to place yourself on thin linguistic ice!

A sign to unbelievers

"Tongues, then, are a sign, not for believers but for unbelievers..." says 1 Corinthians 14:22. It seems unlikely that ecstatic utterances spoken for personal edification would constitute a sign for unbelievers. It is possible, but unlikely. Something as strange and incomprehensible as tongues

---

7 Walter Bauer, *A Greek-English Lexicon of the New Testament*, translators Arndt and Gingrich (Grand Rapids: Zondervan, 1957), 161.

8 Cf. Revelation 5:9; 7:9; 10:11; Acts 2:2, 3, 4, 11, 26.

9 Gundry, p. 299.

speaking would more likely be offensive to them or lead them to the conclusion that the Christian church was a body of madmen!

If an unbeliever had had any contact with tongues speaking, it most likely would have been in the context of the pagan cults that employed ecstatic gibberish. If anything, this would tend to associate the Christian with paganism in the minds of unbelievers. But if a genuine language were being spoken by someone who had never learned it, that could be a sign of the power of God, especially if the message were of the kind found in Acts 2:11, "declaring the wonders of God."

Significant silence

When Paul approaches the subject of tongues in 1 Corinthians 12 he offers no redefinition or clarification of Acts 2. He seems to be assuming that this gift is the universal sign gift that occurred at Pentecost. We have no basis for assuming that he was thinking something else unless he specifically says so.

Paul and Isaiah

Paul specifically states that the tongues of 1 Corinthians 12-14 are foreign languages:

> In the Law it is written, "Through men of strange tongues and through the lips of foreigners I will speak to this people, but even then they will not listen to me," says the Lord (14:21).

Paul is quoting Isaiah 28:11, 12 in which the prophet predicts that a time will come in Israel's history when they will be addressed in Gentile tongues as a sign of God's judgment upon them. Paul says that the tongues of 1 Corinthians 14 are an application of the prediction of Gentile languages.

Don't dabble in babble

In Matthew 6:7 Christ instructs His disciples

21

to avoid meaningless repetition in prayer. The Greek is *battalogesette*. It consists of two parts: *batta*, which is not a word but a sound; and *logeo*, which means "to speak."[10] It has the idea of "to babble, or to speak without thinking."[11] You might translate it, "Don't say, 'batta, batta, batta, batta' when you pray." Jesus is telling His followers not to use the repetition of meaningless sounds as prayer. Speaking in tongues is at times a form of prayer. Would the Holy Spirit cause a believer to utter unknown syllables over and over when the Lord Jesus condemned this practice?

"Interpret" refers to translation from a language

In 1 Corinthians 14:13 Paul says, "For this reason the man who speaks in a tongue should pray that he may interpret what he says." The Greek word translated "interpret" is *diermēneuō*. This verb and its noun form normally refer to the translation of a language and not the explanation of ecstatic speech. Robert Gundry comments, "Although the verb might refer to the explaining of mysterious utterances, its usage in biblical Greek militates against this understanding. Out of 21 uses of *ermēneuō* (apart from the uses in 1 Cor. 12-14) in the LXX and in the New Testament, 18 refer to translation, 2 to explanation, and 1 to satire or a figurative saying."[12]

The language of a foreigner

Notice how Paul specifically says that tongues are foreign languages spoken here on earth in 1 Corinthians 14:10, 11: "Undoubtedly there are all sorts of languages in the world, yet none of them is without meaning. If then I do not grasp

---

10 W. E. Vine, *An Expository Dictionary of New Testament Words* (4 vols. in 1; Westwood: Fleming H. Revell, 1966), III, 281.

11 Bauer, p. 137.

12 Gundry, p. 300.

the meaning of what someone is saying, I am a foreigner to the speaker, and he is a foreigner to me. So it is with you." It is clear that the languages under discussion here in this chapter are those "in the world." Furthermore, the word translated "foreigner" is the Greek word *barbaros,* one who speaks a foreign language known here on earth.

Paul's foregoing comparison between tongues and the sounds of inanimate musical instruments like harps and bugles (1 Cor. 14:7-10) merely implies that from whatever source they come, sounds must be distinct and meaningful. Paul is not suggesting that tongues are non-languages like musical sounds. Rather, the reverse, tongues must be distinctly spoken languages just as a note from a harp or trumpet must be distinct to be effective and meaningful.

In the face of this evidence, we have to conclude that New Testament tongues must have taken the form of meaningful, known words and languages.

WHY TONGUES?

The charismatic movement almost universally holds that the major purpose of the gift of tongues is for personal edification. This is based on two things: first, the statement in 1 Corinthians 14:4 that "he who speaks in a tongue edifies himself," and second, the personal experience of speaking in tongues can be personally edifying. As we begin to search the Scriptures for the purpose of the gift, I think we'll find some strong evidence for a different view.

First, referring to 1 Corinthians 14:4 does not help us in a discussion of the *purpose* of the gift, because what this passage describes is an accompanying product of the exercise of the gift. Any man is edified as he exercises his gift. But we can't say, for example, that because the man who has the gift of evangelism is edified as he evangelizes, the purpose of the gift of evangelism is personal edification. Likewise, the purpose of tongues is not personal edification.

When Paul says that "he who speaks in a tongue edifies himself" he isn't commending the Corinthians for their spirituality! He is actually rebuking them for their misuse of the gift. I think some of the problem may lie in the terseness of Paul's language. To help clear this up, look at 1 Corinthians 11:21. In soundly condemning the Corinthians for their misconduct at the Lord's Supper, Paul puts his criticism this way:

> As you eat, each of you goes ahead without waiting for anybody else. One remains hungry, another gets drunk.

He simply stated what occurred. This is exactly what he is doing in 1 Corinthians 14:4. In both cases he uses a description of their behavior as a rebuke. So we see that Paul is not pleased with speaking in tongues for purely personal edification.

To use any gift for the purpose of personal edification would be a selfish use of the gift. This was part of the abuse of tongues in the Corinthian church. Instead of using their gift for the edification of the body (1 Cor. 12:7), they were using it to edify themselves individually. This is one of the reasons Paul included the love chapter right after chapter 12. In that chapter he says love "...is not self seeking" (1 Cor. 13:5). To use any gift for personal edification is, then, a violation of not only its basic purpose but also the Christian ethic of love. Thus, when Paul says that a man who speaks in tongues edifies himself, he is not saying this by way of commendation but by way of condemnation!

Furthermore, this procedure is common in Paul's teaching method. He starts with where they are (tongues are personally edifying) and then gradually takes them to where they should be (tongues are for a sign against the Jewish nation, 14:21, 22). It is Paul's standard practice to identify with those he is trying to correct in order to get them on "his team" and then to gradually qualify his statement until it almost means the reverse of what he started out to say. For example, in rebuking the Corinthians concerning their tendencies to sexual license he begins by saying, "Everything is permissible for me" (1 Cor. 6:12). This was their statement and Paul agrees with them in the beginning of his rebuke. As his argument advances, however, he says, "Do you not know that he who unites himself to a prostitute is one with her in body?" (1 Cor. 6:16). He then concludes by saying, "Flee from sexual immorality" (6:18). Thus, he began by frankly agreeing with them that all things are permissible under grace. But by the time he has finished he has told them to flee sexual sin! In a similar vein, in 1 Corinthians 14:4, Paul begins where they are (tongues are for personal edification). Then he gradually leads them to realize that this was not the purpose of tongues and in fact was a misuse! Paul desired to be all things to all men and hence he was sensitive to adjust his argument to the emotional temperament of his audience. That is why at first glance he seems to be approving of the use of tongues for personal edification. This teaching methodology is characteristic of Paul and can be illustrated in numerous passages all over the New Testament.[13]

We now have two reasons for believing that the gift of tongues was not intended for personal edification alone. We'll find more reasons as we set forth the evidence for the actual purpose. So what are tongues for?

Sign language

Paul explicitly states the purpose of tongues in 1 Corinthians 14:21, 22:

> In the Law it is written:
> "Through men of strange tongues
> and through the lips of foreigners
> I will speak to this people,
> but even then they will not listen to me,"
> says the Lord.
> Tongues, then, are a sign, not for believers but for unbelievers.

So tongues are a sign to unbelievers. The word translated "for" is the Greek preposition *eis* which here indicates purpose.[14] Thus, Paul is stating not merely that tongues are a sign, but they were intended to be such. This particular expression is used ten times in the Greek Old Testament, the Septuagint (i.e., *for a sign*), and in each instance it is a distinct statement of purpose.[15] We have therefore a definite statement of the purpose of tongues. It is a sign for unbelievers.

Furthermore, Paul is quoting a passage in the Old Testament, Isaiah 28:11, 12, as we noted be-

---

13 H. Chadwick, "All Things to All Men," *New Testament Studies*, May 1955, Vol. 1, pp. 261-275. Dr. Chadwick does an excellent job of presenting Paul's teaching methodology on this point and gives many helpful illustrations. Also in this connection see D. W. B. Robinson, "Charismata versus Pneumatika: Paul's Method of Discussion," *The Reformed Theological Review*, May-Aug., 1972, pp. 49-55.

14 H. E. Dama and Julius R. Mantey, *A Manual Grammar of the Greek New Testament* (New York: The Macmillan Co., 1955), p. 104.

15 Genesis 1:14; 9:13; Exodus 13:16; 20:12; 20:20; Numbers 17:3; Joshua 4:6; Isaiah 8:18; 19:20; 55:13.

fore, which speaks of tongues specifically as a judicial sign against "this people." In context that refers to Judah, the Jews. Putting these two statements together, we come to the conclusion that tongues are specifically a sign for unbelieving Jews.

In order to understand this more clearly, it will be helpful to take a brief look at the Isaiah 28 passage. The context is set in the latter years of King Hezekiah of Judah (705-701 B.C.). In 722 B.C. the Assyrians had invaded Palestine and destroyed the Northern Kingdom, called Israel or Ephraim. In 705 B.C. Isaiah is warning the rulers of the Southern Kingdom, Judah, that the same thing that happened to Israel (28:1-6), can happen to Judah (28:7-15). The rulers of Judah are being rebuked by Isaiah because instead of trusting in the Lord to deliver Judah from Assyria, they are trusting in an alliance they made with the Egyptians (28:15; 30:1, 2; 31:1). In 28:7, 8, Isaiah comes upon the leaders of Judah while they are involved in a drunken party. He says,

> And these also reel with wine and stagger from strong drink,
> The priest and the prophet reel with strong drink,
> They are confused by wine, they stagger from strong drink;
> They reel while having visions,
> They totter when rendering judgment.
> For all the tables are full of filthy vomit, without a single clean place (Isa. 28:7, 8).

In other words, Isaiah is calling them a bunch of filthy drunken bums! Understandably, they don't appreciate his attitude and they begin to sneer at the prophet and his teachings in the next verses. They call his teachings simple and childish. He has been instructing them as if they were infants. They say,

> To whom would he teach knowledge?

27

> And to whom would he interpret the message?
> Those just weaned from milk?
> Those just taken from the breast? (28:9).

They are sneering at Isaiah as if he were an intolerable moralist.[16] They are of age and free, and he doesn't need to bring any knowledge to them. "Does Isaiah think we are babies? His teachings are for children." In the next verse they begin to ridicule the simplistic nature of his teaching.

> For he says,
> Order on order, order on order,
> Line on line, line on line,
> A little here, a little there (28:10).

They regard his message as boringly simple and repetitive. Isaiah now replies to their scorn in verses 11-13 with an announcement of coming judgment. These are the verses quoted by the Apostle Paul and applied to the tongues question in first-century Corinth. Isaiah replies that since they would not listen when God spoke to them simply and plainly in Hebrew, God will now speak to them in a language that they cannot understand, i.e., Assyrian.

> Indeed, He will speak to this people
> Through stammering lips and a foreign tongue
> (28:11).

The language of the Assyrian invaders had a rather jarring effect on Jewish ears.

Thus, because of their unbelief and apostasy, God is going to bring a judgment on them. The judgment involves the sign of tongues. They will not understand what is being said to them. The notion of being addressed in "other tongues" was a common theme of judgment in the Old Testament. In Deuteronomy 28:15-68 (see 28:49) Moses foretold the coming invasion of Palestine in A.D.

---

16 Franz Delitzsch, *Isaiah* (2 vols.; Grand Rapids: Eerdmans, n.d.), II, 6.

28

70. He specifically notes that a part of that invasion involved being subjected to a language that they could not understand. The same concept is mentioned in Jeremiah 5:15. To be addressed in other tongues was a symbol of judgment to the Hebrew mind. It meant they hadn't listened when God spoke to them in Hebrew so He was now going to speak to them in languages they could not understand. So the sign of tongues in Isaiah was not a saving sign to convince the Jews, but was intended to be a judicial sign announcing that because of their hardened hearts they would not listen, so God will now veil His truth from them.

We are now in a better position to understand why Paul applied this passage in Isaiah to the Corinthian church in 1 Corinthians 14:21, 22. Unknown languages were considered a sign of judgment. In Isaiah's time God had pronounced judgment on Judah. He summoned the Assyrians speaking in Gentile languages as a sign of judgment. The Jewish people were once again in apostasy in the first century A.D. and again, Paul says, God was bringing the sign of tongues as a sign of judgment. The period of Jewish favor as a nation had passed. Their rejection of their Messiah left the nation under the judgment of God, a judgment which was executed through the invasion of Titus and the Roman legions in A.D. 70 with the utter destruction of Jerusalem and the dispersion of the Jewish people.

As soon as the Jews heard the gift of tongues being manifested in the assemblies of the followers of Jesus and at Pentecost, they should have been warned that the nation was under judgment and they had better repent. But even though they saw the miraculous sign of tongues, and knew

that it spoke of judgment, and knew that it testified to the reality of the new age, they still would
not listen. Paul says,

> Through men of strange tongues
>   and through the lips of foreigners
> I will speak to this people,
>   but even then they will not listen to me
> (1 Cor. 14:21).

Paul has quoted Isaiah 28:11 but modified the
quote slightly. In so doing he emphasizes the
greater degree of apostasy in the first century. In
Isaiah 28:11 the sign of tongues came as a judgment because they would not listen in Hebrew.
In the Corinthians passage, tongues again came as
a judgment sign, and again for not listening to
Christ in their native tongue, but even after hearing and seeing the gift of tongues manifested to
signify their apostasy, Israel *still* will not listen!

Thus, Paul is quoting the Isaiah passage to
draw a principle out and apply it to the tongues
question in the first century. The principle is that
tongues were used in the Old Testament for a
sign of judgment and that is their purpose in the
New. They are not for personal edification! So
1 Corinthians 14:21 is not a fulfillment of the
prophecy of Isaiah 28:11 but is an illustration of
a general principle to which that prophecy testifies, i.e., tongues are a sign of judgment.

Robertson and Plummer concur in this interpretation. "Tongues have a further use, as a sign
to *un*believers; not a convincing, saving sign, but
a judicial sign. Just as the disobedient Jews who
refused to listen to the clear and intelligible message which God frequently sent to them through
His prophets, were chastised by being made to
listen to the unintelligible language of a foreign
invader, so those who now fail to believe the Gospel are chastised by hearing wonderful sounds

which they cannot understand. If this is correct, we may compare Christ's use of parables to veil His meaning from those who could not or would not receive it."[17] Findlay comments, "God spoke to Israel through the strange Assyrian tongue *in retribution,* not to confirm their faith but to consummate their unbelief."[18] He adds that the logical connection of thought that connects 1 Corinthians 14:21, and 22 "...forbids the thought of a convincing and a saving sign."[19]

If tongues are a sign of judgment, we should find that evident whenever tongues appear in the New Testament record. So let's check the Book of Acts. Although the purpose of the gift is never stated in Acts itself, Paul tells us in 1 Corinthians 14:21, 22 that it served as a judicial sign in the events of Acts.

In Acts 2 there were many unbelievers present. The sign of tongues came as proof that the outpouring of the Spirit had come even though Israel as a nation was not the instrument through which it was mediated. Thus God was now operating outside the nation Israel, and the tongues phenomenon showed clearly that God was now bypassing Israel and that the nation was now under judgment for their rejection of the Messiah.

Peter announced that Israel was under judgment in Acts 2, and the sign gifts of the Spirit were the authenticating factors, confirming that he was right:

> Therefore, let all Israel be assured of this: God has made this Jesus whom you crucified both Lord and Christ (Acts 2:36).

---

[17] Robertson and Plummer, *The International Critical Commentary, I Corinthians* (Edinburgh: T & T Clark, 1914), p. 316.
[18] G. G. Findlay, *St. Paul's First Epistle to the Corinthians: The Expositor's Greek Testament,* ed. W. Robertson Nicoll (5 vols.; Grand Rapids: Eerdmans, 1967), II, 910.
[19] Ibid., p. 910.

Here Peter is asserting that Israel is now under judgment for the crucifixion of the Messiah and that they are in need of repentance.

In Acts 8 and 10 there seems at first to be a problem in that there were no unbelievers present, though Paul says that the gift was for those who do not believe. But think about it: Israel as a nation would hear what happened and they would read it in the New Testament Scriptures for centuries. For nearly two thousand years the events of Acts 2, 8, 10 and 19 have stood as a sign to the nation that God has bypassed them. God is now including their most hated enemies, Gentiles, in His plan and purpose. The fact that there were no unbelievers actually present during the events becomes irrelevant. Romans 9-11 gives the theology behind all this, but the gift of tongues is the sign that it has taken place.

Look at this parallel: the sign of the resurrection of Christ was given only to believers. Only believers saw Him resurrected with their own eyes. Nevertheless it was used as a sign for unbelievers, through the eyewitness testimony of believers. Likewise it is not necessary that unbelievers be present every time the gift of tongues is manifested in order for that gift to serve as a judicial sign against them.

In Acts 8 some Samaritans receive the gift, thereby showing that they are on an equal basis with the Jewish converts of Acts 2, and that Israel is no longer the people through whom God is going to work, at least for a period of time. The giving of the gift of tongues to Gentiles in Acts 10 showed that Gentiles were on an equal basis with the Jewish converts. To say that Samaritans and Gentiles are now in the center of God's plan is to say that Israel is not and hence as a nation is under judgment.

In a similar way the tongues of Acts 19 announced that the "new age" had begun. Tongues identified the Jews in Acts 19 with the Jews in Acts 2, the Samaritans in Acts 8 and the Gentiles in Acts 10, constituting further proof that God was now operating outside of the nation of Israel.

The disciples in Ephesus in Acts 19 were a long way from Jerusalem, where the capital of the Messianic age was supposed to be located (Isa. 2). Thus Acts 19 serves as a sign to the unbelieving nation that the nation is no longer the center of God's program. His purpose is being worked out hundreds of miles away from Jerusalem; that city is not the center any more.

Apostolic authority

The second use of tongues as a sign concerned the apostles and their new authority. The gift of tongues served to validate both the apostles and their message to Israel:

> The things that mark an apostle — signs, wonders, and miracles — were done among you with great perseverance (2 Cor. 12:12).

> God also testified to it by signs, wonders and various miracles, and gifts of the Holy Spirit distributed according to his will (Heb. 2:4).

> By the power of signs and miracles, through the power of the Spirit . . . (Rom. 15:19).

In Acts 2, 8, 10 and 19 the gift of tongues served to validate the apostolic authority of Peter and Paul through whom the gift was imparted. By validating their message, the gift of tongues served in turn as a sign of judgment on Israel. God was no longer working through the high priests and the synagogue; the apostles were the new authorities and the body of Christ was the new synagogue. The apostles' message condemned Israel

33

and the gift of tongues confirmed the apostles. Therefore the gift of tongues condemned Israel.

Salvation for individuals

Tongues also served as a sign for *individual* Jews that the new church age had begun, and that they now could personally embrace Jesus of Nazareth as Messiah, thus receiving salvation individually outside of the synagogue.

Individual Jews responded to Peter's message which had been authenticated by the gift of tongues; we are told that three thousand believed (Acts 2:41). The fact that men were finding salvation outside of the synagogue constituted a judicial act against Israel on the part of the Holy Spirit. The presence of the gift of tongues among some believers served as an authenticating sign that the Holy Spirit was working outside of Israel and consequently that Israel was now under judgment.

Today we sometimes hear of isolated instances in which tongues have served to overcome unbelief, even Jewish unbelief.[20] No one who knows Christ would doubt that this has happened. What we are questioning is not what has happened in a few isolated instances, but the general trend of the charismatic movement as a whole. Within the movement the usage of tongues as a sign is not at all central, and as a sign to overcome Jewish unbelief is almost totally absent. In any case, tongues were a judicial sign and not a saving sign.

We have seen three main purposes of the gift of tongues in the New Testament: as a sign to unbelieving Jews, as a sign authenticating the apostles, and as an announcement that individual salvation was now offered through Jesus. All three

20 Author not mentioned. "Speaking with Other Tongues," *The Pentecostal Evangel*, No. 2607, April 1964, p. 3.

of these uses served in turn as a judicial sign against Israel. But there is a fourth purpose, which might also be considered a product of the first three uses, and which is important in deciding the place of tongues in the church today.

The Bible consistently says that the primary use of tongues was not for the church but for use outside the church as a sign to unbelievers. Then we find Paul in 1 Corinthians 14 urging that tongues used in the church be interpreted so that the whole assembly might profit. Now how could a judicial sign against unbelievers be of value to the church body? Scripture gives some answers.

Edifying the body

The Scriptures clearly teach that the purpose of all the gifts in general and the gift of tongues in particular is for the edification of the church as a whole and not for the individual. In what way did the gift of tongues edify the early church?

First, tongues edified the early church by preventing the future establishment of a Jewish church versus a Samaritan church versus a Gentile church. The giving of the gift to the Samaritans in Acts 8 and the Gentiles at Caesarea in Acts 10 prevented the age-old divisions between Jews, Samaritans, and Gentiles from being perpetrated in the church of God. Acts 11:15-18 describes what happened, and we'll delve into that in chapter 4.

We can see that the gift of tongues was extremely edifying in that it was an aid to church unity. This becomes rather ironic when we remember that the church at Corinth was one of the most fractured churches Paul ever dealt with! Also ironic—and regrettable—has been the divisive effect of the appearance of tongues within the Christian church today. This has not been entirely the fault of the tongues speakers; hasty and unloving responses from non-tongues speakers have contributed to the splintering.

The second way in which tongues edified the early church was through their authenticating of the apostles and their message, as we already mentioned. Through the gift of tongues God put His own stamp on the apostles and their message, confirming to first-century Christians that these men and their message were of God and were to be received as bearers of the truth. Thus in the critical first years of the new faith God made sure that only true apostles and true doctrine would be accepted by young believers.

Also important in the edification of the church was the role of tongues as an identifying mark. The gift helped give the infant church an independent identity in the face of the overwhelming size and age of Judaism. At first Christianity was considered another Jewish sect; then, as believers began to speak in tongues, it became a sign announcing that God's favor toward Israel had passed and that He now was beginning a new body, the body of Christ. In this way believers were established in an identity separate from Israel. This is important psychologically for a new faith. It also would make the break from centuries of traditional Judaism a little easier for Jewish converts if they had some outward sign available to confirm to their hearts that they had made the right decision.

Next, tongues served to edify the church in at least one instance by adding numbers to the body. In Acts 2 the appearance of tongues at Pentecost seems to have been a factor in convincing some non-Christians that the Gospel was true. Thus the church was literally edified or "built up" in that three thousand converts were added to it. However, I believe that in God's purpose this benefit of the gift was not at all primary but incidental.

And last, tongues when translated became prophecy and thus were edifying to the believers gathered in the assembly. I don't feel that tongues were primarily intended for use in the assembly, but when so used Paul required that they be interpreted so that the whole church might benefit. So we can see that even though the sign of tongues was a judicial sign against unbelieving Israel, in performing this function it served for the edification of the church as all the gifts were intended to do. Consider the following Scriptures:

> Now to each man the manifestation of the Spirit is given for the common good (1 Cor. 12:7).

Paul then goes on to list various manifestations that are for the common good. This list includes tongues, so we have another specific statement of the purpose of tongues.

> Since you are eager to have spiritual gifts, try to excel in gifts that build up the church (1 Cor. 14:12).

In the above passage Paul is emphasizing that if the gift of tongues is to be used in the church, which is not its primary purpose, it should be used for the edification of the church as a whole. He explains this in the following verse:

> For this reason the man who speaks in a tongue should pray that he may interpret what he says (v. 13).

The church at Corinth was abusing the gift of tongues, using it for personal edification instead of for the building up of the body. The whole point of 1 Corinthians 12-14 is to argue against the use of tongues in personal devotion to praise God and thereby receive purely personal upbuilding.

Ephesians 4:11, 12 reads:

> It was he who gave some to be apostles, some to be prophets, some to be evangelists, and some to be pastors and teachers, to prepare God's people for works of service, so that the body of Christ may be built up.

This refers to Christ's giving of gifted men to the church. These men were to use their gifts for the edifying of the total body. This is a purpose clause in the Greek and it is followed by two other purpose clauses in verses 13 and 14. In these verses also the purpose of the gifts is specifically stated to be the building up of the whole body and not personal edification.

Does motive make a difference?

"But," you may be asking, "can't I use tongues for personal devotions as long as selfish motives are not the major emphasis?" That's a good question. The Bible provides us with some answers.

Just between Thee and me

Passages such as 1 Corinthians 14:28 seem to indicate that Paul recognized some kind of private conversation between a person and God:

> If there is no interpreter, the speaker should keep quiet in the church and speak to himself and God.

We need to note right away that it is not at all certain that Paul is referring to speaking in tongues when he mentions speaking to oneself and God. In fact, in view of Paul's earlier injunction that prayer without an interpreter causes the mind to be unfruitful (1 Cor. 14:14), doesn't it seem unlikely that he now would approve of a means of prayer that he considered to be unprofitable?

Even if we take the other interpretation and say that Paul *is* allowing a private devotional use for tongues in this passage, we would have to conclude that it simply is by way of permission and not at all a recommendation. There are a number of Scriptures that seem to prohibit the private use of tongues for devotional purposes.

Repetition reprimanded

Matthew 6:7:

> And when you pray, do not keep on babbling like pagans, for they think they will be heard because of their many words.

As we saw before, the Greek word translated "babbling" refers to repeating syllables without thinking. It refers to prayer in which the mind is not engaged. Can we really say that a person praying in tongues has his mind engaged? This command seems to prohibit personal devotional prayer in ecstatic utterances. It also would prohibit prayer in the genuine gift of tongues, foreign languages, unless the person praying understands what he is saying.

The key thought of the word *battalogesette* ("babble") is of prayer without engaging the mind. As pointed out earlier (page 13) Paul also forbids prayer without the engagement of the mind in 1 Corinthians 14:13-15. There he insists that he will pray with the spirit but he will include his mind. That is, he will not pray unless he understands what he is praying! Why did Jesus forbid private prayer without the engagement of the mind? What real harm is done if a person wants to go to his closet and let his mind go blank and then begin to utter ecstatic utterances or even foreign languages to God? Many testify to the feeling of worship and closeness to God and the sensation that they are communicating more effectively and at a deeper level than they do when they speak in their native tongue to God.

Consider from this perspective what Jesus says in Matthew 6:7, "...for they think they will be heard *because* of their many words." It was the pagan notion that the deity heard you when you prayed without the mind being engaged. The pagans felt that they were communicating more effectively when they spoke many words in ecstatic utterances with their minds being passive. Isn't this exactly what many of our charismatic brethren are telling us today? The pagans believed that the "spirit" had direct access to the deity through their passive minds and hence could pray for them. Thus, the intermediate human mind was bypassed and direct communication was supposedly established.

Notice, Jesus says that men who pray without their minds being engaged think that they are being heard *because* they are praying this way. In other words, they tend to approach God on the basis of a certain kind of prayer rather than on the basis of the cross of Christ. Instead of coming in "Jesus' name," they stand on the basis of *battalogesette!* Your access, your communication, your intimacy to the Lord Jesus can be increased by a work, i.e., a certain kind of prayer. It is curious in this regard, that in many charismatic healing meetings the afflicted is prayed for in tongues rather than in English. Is this because they think they are more likely to be heard if they speak in tongues than if they speak in English? I remember as a young believer, becoming involved in the healing of a young woman who had cancer. The Christian brother who had "the gift of healing" prayed for her in tongues rather than in English and we all laid hands on her head. She died six months later. He thought that he would be heard because of his many words of *battalogesette*. Thus, God hears us more thoroughly and is more likely to answer our prayers if we pray in tongues than if we pray in English!

This is a law system of prayer. We stand before God on the basis of the shed blood of Christ and not the particular form of prayer we adopt. To think there is more intimate communication going on when you speak in tongues is a delusion. Furthermore, in the lives of some it could lead to a dangerous notion that God accepts us, hears us, answers our prayers, etc., in response to works instead of faith and grace. I can't examine the inner life of our charismatic brethren, but possibly it was this danger that moved the Lord to forbid prayer without the mind engaged.

"Teach us to pray..."

When Christ taught His disciples in Matthew 6:9-13 to pray He did not teach them to pray in an unknown tongue. He gave them a model prayer in their own language. Should we conclude that a prayer which we don't understand can be superior to the prayer our Lord taught us? When we pray in ecstatic utterances or in the genuine gift of tongues we don't understand what we are saying, and thus are not praying according to the pattern that Christ gave us.

Pray for specifics

The Bible teaches us to pray for specific things, such as food (Matt. 6:11), forgiveness of sins (Matt. 6:12), wisdom (James 1:5), and strength (Eph. 3:16). When someone prays in tongues he doesn't know what he is praying for. In fact, if he doesn't know what he is praying for, how can he be certain that he is praying at all?

Does God speak English?

When we get right down to it, what is the purpose of praying in tongues devotionally? God understands your native language as well as your unknown tongue, so it has no different effect on

God. Furthermore, according to Paul, it is not as fruitful for you as prayer in which your mind is engaged.

Summing up

Scripture seems to indicate that the genuine gift of tongues consists of foreign languages, and that God's major purpose of the gift was as a sign to the nation of Israel. Proper use of the gift resulted in the edification of the whole church. With this in mind, can we still try to use tongues today for personal devotional prayer?

Many believers today feel that using tongues in this way is the gateway to a fuller, more powerful walk and witness. Let's see if this is borne out through Scripture and church history.

2

The baptism of the Holy Spirit: What is it, what good is it, and how can I know if I have it?

This is an age of experience! Old norms have come crumbling down, and our society is in a state of flux in which there is no longer right and wrong, good and evil. Anti-hero movies tell us that the bad guys are really the good guys and the good guys are good only for laughs. Numerous television shows depict divorce, abortion, and the occult as part of everyday life. New "religions" such as Mind Control and Alpha state meditation are replacing Christianity. Situation ethics reigns; everything depends. When no one has any absolute answers any more (that's "narrow" and "primitive"), everything depends on you the individual and your situation and your experience.

In this sea of uncertainty, our human hearts grope for an anchor of absoluteness. What is really true and valid? How can I know anything for sure? On what can I build my life?

The Christian church has not escaped this sea of relativism. New theological fads come and go like corks bobbing on the waves. (Whatever happened to the "God Is Dead" movement?) This tossing about by every wind of doctrine is bound to happen when pastors and teachers abandon the historic truths of the Bible. Serious study of the Bible has become obsolete for many because "there are so many interpretations." Thus, being squeezed into the mold of our age, many Christians are relying on experience as the ultimate criterion for truth. The charismatic movement offers such an experience, the "baptism in the Holy Spirit." Many people seeking the truth grasp onto this apparently miraculous experience, believing that they have found their anchor.

Let's look at the "baptism" offered by the charismatic movement, and then at the baptism described in Scripture. Let's see what are the supposed and real benefits, and what is the real test of having received the Holy Spirit.

What Is the "Baptism"?

"The baptism in the Holy Spirit is a second encounter with God (the first is conversion) in which the Christian begins to receive the supernatural power of the Holy Spirit into his life.... The Christian is brought into a deeper relationship with Christ."[1] This definition by a leading charismatic writer and speaker would find agreement among most charismatics today.

There are seven passages that refer to the baptism with the Holy Spirit: Matthew 3:11; Mark 1:8; Luke 3:16; John 1:33; Acts 1:5; 11:6; and 1 Corinthians 12:13. Only one, 1 Corinthians 12:13, gives a definition of the baptism: "For we were all baptized by one Spirit into one body...."

Charismatics hold that there are two different functions referred to in Scripture as the "baptism of the Holy Spirit." They often make a distinction between passages such as Acts 1:5, which reads "baptized *with* the Holy Spirit," and 1 Corinthians 12:13, "baptized *by* one Spirit." This is done to support their contention that the Holy Spirit acts to place the believer in the body of

1 Don Basham, *A Handbook on Holy Spirit Baptism* (Reading, Berkshire, England: Gateway Outreach; Dist. in U.S. by Holy Spirit Teaching Mission, 1730 S.W. 22nd Avenue, Fort Lauderdale, Florida 33312, 1969), p. 10.

Christ at the point of salvation, but that the fullness of the Holy Spirit must be received at a later time. In the words of the same charismatic writer: "Certainly the Holy Spirit is present in conversion. Every Christian experiences a measure of the Holy Spirit's power. But the Scriptures plainly teach there is spiritual power available beyond our experience of conversion.... The baptism in the Holy Spirit is *receiving* Him with power into our lives."[2]

One small preposition should settle this. The Greek word *en* could be translated as "by," "with," or "in." This word is used in every passage of the New Testament where the baptism *en* the Spirit is mentioned. So however you translate it, you should translate it the same way every time. But whether you call it baptism by the Spirit, with the Spirit, or in the Spirit, 1 Corinthians 12:13 clearly teaches what baptism *en* the Spirit is: a ministry performed by God, in which He places the believer into the body of Christ. No other passage gives us any other definition.

WHAT ARE THE BENEFITS?

First let's get our thinking straight about an issue both charismatics and non-charismatics tend to be fuzzy on. Is it the Holy Spirit or the gift of tongues that is supposed to provide power and a deeper walk? To those who say "tongues" there is this reply:

(1) If the gift of tongues results in greater power, why is it that the church at Corinth was the most carnal church that Paul ever dealt with? To answer that the Corinthians simply were abusing the gift only serves to weaken the argument. The gift does not produce spirituality automati-

---

2 Ibid., p. 12.

cally. In fact, the only tongues-speaking church that we read of in the epistles was a carnal, divided church (1 Cor. 3:1-4).

(2) There isn't a single passage in the Bible that specifically says that tongues are the source of greater spirituality, while there are many that say that the receiving of the Spirit does have this result. Some believers identify the receiving of the Spirit so closely with the gift of tongues that they come to regard tongues as the source of new power, often quoting Acts 2 to support their position.

(3) Throughout church history the greatest movements and revivals have had no association with nor emphasis on tongues. Moody, Finney, Luther, Calvin, and others give no emphasis on speaking in tongues. In fact, an outbreak of charismatic manifestations almost destroyed the impact of the Reformation, and caused Luther to speak out against such things. Emphasis on "private revelations" had led many to religious fanaticism and a lack of discernment in many areas. Luther gently and lovingly turned believers away from this.

(4) Jesus never spoke in tongues. The Spirit descended upon Him at His baptism, but there is no evidence that He ever spoke in tongues. Some may argue that Jesus had perfect fellowship with the Father and had no need for praying to Him in tongues, though we do. But Jesus either lived or taught everything we need to do in our Christian life. Though He was in constant fellowship with the Father He spent long hours in prayer. Though He had no need to confess sin He taught His disciples to do it. If we were to need tongues speaking in our Christian walk, doesn't it seem that Christ also would have taught us that?

Tongues do not give new power, but the baptism of the Holy Spirit does! It is my conviction that the Bible teaches that all of this power is given to every believer at the point in time when he believes. At that time the baptism places us in Christ and we become the possessors of "every spiritual blessing in Christ" (Eph. 1:3).

But, you say, you know many people who already were believers, whose lives were changed for the better when they began to speak in tongues. I, too, personally know many believers whose lives were affected in this way. If tongues do not bring greater power to the believer's life, then how do we explain these people's experiences? Some partial answers:

(1) Often there is much genuine seeking of the Lord prior to or after the experience of tongues speaking. God tells us that we will surely find Him when we search for Him with all our heart (Jer. 29:13).

(2) There often is an emphasis on prayer, with much time being spent speaking with God. Jesus spent much time in prayer, and the Bible commands us to pray continually (Luke 18:1; 1 Thess. 5:17).

(3) If a Christian has sought honestly to be more Spirit-filled than he was before, and has yielded himself more completely to the Spirit's promptings, this is bound to bring spiritual rewards. We are commanded to have our mind controlled by the Spirit (Rom. 8:6), to be led by the Spirit (Gal. 5:18), and to live according to God in the Spirit (1 Pet. 4:6).

(4) When a person begins to speak in tongues in a small group, this usually is the culmination of a time of Christian fellowship, Bible study, and prayer in a closely knit circle of spiritually minded friends (though this is not always the case). Such

an experience is bound to be profitable.[3] The writer to the Hebrews admonishes us to get together for fellowship: "Let us not give up meeting together...but let us encourage one another..." (Heb. 10:25).

When we fulfill all the conditions for God's promises, should we be surprised that He answers and blesses us? When we obey His commands as given in Scripture we should expect Him to honor His Word and draw near to us. But will we instead choose to disregard the simple black-and-white promises and attribute the blessing to something else?

How Can I Be Sure I Have It?

After speaking at a conference on marriage and the family, I received a letter from a couple who had attended. They expressed their appreciation for the messages, and then related how after the conference they had received the "baptism." Moved, I'm sure, by genuine concern for my spiritual growth, they asked, "Have you received the baptism?" What they meant was, "Have you spoken in tongues?" Most charismatics regard speaking in tongues as the primary evidence of the baptism of the Holy Spirit, some going so far as to claim that tongues are the only scriptural evidence.[4] Does this claim hold up in the light of the New Testament?

We find in 1 Corinthians 12:30 the question, "Do all speak with tongues?" The way the question is worded in the Greek indicates that a negative answer is expected: "No, not all speak with tongues."[5] Couple this with 1 Corinthians 12:13

---

3 Anthony Hoekema, *What About Tongues Speaking?* (Grand Rapids: Eerdmans, 1966), p. 136.

4 Basham, p. 61.

5 Walter Bauer, *A Greek-English Lexicon of the New Testa-*

and the problem seems to dissolve. In 1 Corinthians 12:13 we read that *all* have been baptized with the Spirit, and 1 Corinthians 12:30 states that *not all* speak with tongues. So speaking in tongues can't be the sign of the baptism of the Spirit.⌝

Those who try to evade the force of this by stating that what Paul is referring to in verse 30 is speaking in tongues in the church assembly are twisting the context to fit their experience.[6] Though Paul is addressing them as a church, it doesn't necessarily follow that this refers to the church in assembly. In fact, to interpret it in that way would violate the context, as follows:

(1) The statement wouldn't make much sense. The other things listed by Paul are not the possession of all members of the church (the gifts of apostleship, prophecy, teaching, healing, government, etc.).

(2) The conclusion that all do speak with tongues in private even if they don't in the assembly would have to be applied, if we're going to be consistent, to the other items in the list also. This would mean that all are apostles privately though all are not apostles in the assembly; all have the gift of government privately, though not all have the gift in the assembly. I think it is obvious that not all are apostles, nor do all govern, and so on.

(3) The whole thrust of the context is to help believers recognize the individuality of the gifts. They are not to be anxious if they do not have as important a gift as someone else. To inject the thought into verse 30 that the reference there is only to the exercise of the gift in the public assem-

ment. Translated by William F. Arndt and F. Wilbur Gingrich (Grand Rapids: Zondervan, 1957), p. 519.

6 Victor Paul Wierwille, *Receiving the Holy Spirit Today* (New Knoxville, Ohio: The Way, Inc., 1967), pp. 167, 168.

bly is to remove the force of the context and to make the preceding argument irrelevant. Paul would be saying, "Don't be upset if you don't exercise your gift in the assembly while someone else does; you can exercise it in private." This would be out of harmony with the whole force and context of the chapter.

May I suggest that the New Testament teaches that the evidences of having been baptized with the Holy Spirit are not miraculous but moral, not ecstatic but ethical! There are seven, not one, basic evidences given in the Bible by which you can examine your life to see if you truly have the gift of the Spirit.

Praying to God as your Father

"Because you are sons, God sent the Spirit of his Son into our hearts, the Spirit who calls out, 'Abba, Father'" (Gal. 4:6).

"For you did not receive a spirit that makes you a slave again to fear, but you received the Spirit who makes you sons. And by him we cry, 'Abba, Father.' The Spirit himself testifies with our spirit that we are God's children" (Rom. 8:15, 16).

The first evidence is that you are able to pray to God as your Father. This is Christian prayer. It's not very flashy but it's biblical!

An understanding of the grace of God

One of the first things that comes to your consciousness after you have been given the gift of the Holy Spirit is the realization of God's unmerited favor bestowed upon you. You begin to develop an increasing degree of appreciation for the wisdom of God in providing salvation through the cross. You realize how much you don't deserve salvation, and how great is God's unmerited blessing toward us in Christ. This is what Paul is speaking about when he says, "We have not received the spirit of the world but the Spirit who is from God, that we may understand what God has freely given us" (1 Cor. 2:12). "What God has freely given us" — that is grace! Without the Spirit we have no understanding of this grace.

A consciousness of the love of God

Paul tells us, "And hope does not disappoint us, because God has poured out his love into our hearts by the Holy Spirit, whom he has given us" (Rom. 5:5). One of the things you sense for the first time after you receive the Spirit is that God loves you. I don't mean a vague, misty feeling that Someone somewhere cares about the human race, but an undeniable conviction that a personal God actually *loves you,* on a one-to-one basis.

An assurance of salvation

A "guarantee" of eternal life is one product of the Holy Spirit's working: "(God) set his seal of ownership on us, and put his Spirit in our hearts as a deposit, guaranteeing what is to come" (2 Cor. 1:22). We feel assured of salvation.

We should point out that a lack of that sense of guarantee or a lack of one or more of these evidences does not necessarily imply that one is not a Christian, that he has not received the Spirit. It could also be that Satan is accusing him, or that there are some guilt or psychological problems that are quenching the Spirit's voice.

A confession of the ordinary and the human Jesus

The apostle John wrote, "This is how you can recognize the Spirit of God: Every spirit that acknowledges that Jesus Christ has come in the flesh is from God, but every spirit that does not acknowledge Jesus is not from God..." (1 John 4:2, 3).

"Well," you say, "many people today believe that Jesus came in a human body, and many of them are outright atheists! How, then, can this be a test of the presence of the Spirit?"

John was writing to deal with a particular problem: during the latter part of the first century the Christian church was plagued by a group called Gnostics. These Gnostics claimed to be the recipients of a higher knowledge *(gnosis)* that enabled them to walk in a more intimate union with God than did other believers. They placed a special emphasis on mystical, "spiritual" experiences. One of their central teachings was that Jesus' body was either only a ghost or incidental and very unimportant. The spirit of Jesus was the most important thing to them. Hence they would speak of the human Jesus and the divine Christ, but never of Jesus Christ as having a literal body. These false teachers sounded very spiritual because they always emphasized the spirit over the body and the mystical over the ordinary.

It was against this background that John wrote his first letter. Because we are not facing Gnostics today, this passage has no *direct* application to us. Today there are indeed many who would confess that Jesus Christ came in the flesh, but that doesn't mean that they are from God. I have heard Christian brothers use this verse as a way of proving that their "gift of tongues" is from God. When asked, as a test, if Jesus came in the flesh, they responded in tongues. The interpretation of the tongue would turn out to be something like, "Jesus Christ came in the flesh."

But this test and this kind of confession were valid only against the context in which John was applying it, against the Gnostic false teachers. This confession would definitely have surfaced a Gnostic heretic because that was the very point he didn't believe! But it would prove nothing today unless we were faced with the same heresy.

However, there are two particular parallels between Gnosticism and the charismatic movement to which I think this passage might apply. First, the Gnostics made a distinction between what they called the psychic or ordinary Christian, and the pneumatic or spirit-filled Christian, with levels in between based on "higher experiences."[7] The pneumatic Christians considered themselves to be on a higher level, and were more mystical and more "spiritual" than others. The distinction which the charismatics often draw between the "ordinary" Christian and the "spirit-filled" Christian seems to parallel this tendency.

Second, the Gnostic maintained that the evidence of whether you had become pneumatic consisted in certain "miraculous" and "higher" experiences. But this was exactly what was central in all of the pagan mystery religions: in these cults speaking in tongues was the evidence that you had moved up to a higher state. This is the same thing that occurs in the modern charismatic movement. You move up spiritually when you experience the "baptism," tongues, and a deepening of your walk; deeper is higher!

The emphasis on the outward and more "miraculous" in the pagan religions and in Gnosticism parallels modern charismatic emphasis. John is countering this by declaring that the real evidence of the presence of the Holy Spirit is His testimony to the ordinary, the fleshly Christ. John is saying simply that the real evidence of the gift of the Spirit is practical, down to earth, everyday Christi-

---

[7] Reinhold Seeberg, *History of Doctrine* (Grand Rapids: Baker Book House 1964), p. 98.

53

anity. This evidence actually is more of a warning as to what does *not* indicate the presence of the Spirit: the thing that John says is evidence of the absence of the Spirit, the Gnostics and many modern charismatics say is evidence of His presence.

The fruit of the Spirit

The sixth line of evidence that the New Testament gives is found in Galatians 5:22, 23: "But the fruit of the Spirit is love, joy, peace, patience, kindness, goodness, faithfulness, gentleness, and self-control...." According to Paul, you will experience a new quality of life. Do you find the above qualities becoming more and more apparent in yourself? If you do, that is evidence that you have received the baptism in the Holy Spirit.

The absence of these characteristics doesn't necessarily indicate the absence of the Spirit. It could be instead evidence of immaturity (1 Cor. 3:1) or carnality (1 Cor. 3:1-4).

Love for other Christians

Perhaps the most significant evidence that we have received the Holy Spirit is a new love in our hearts for our brothers and sisters in Christ. Consider the words of the apostle John: "No one has ever seen God; but if we love each other, God lives in us and his love is made complete in us. We know that we live in him and he in us, because he has given us of his Spirit" (1 John 4:12, 13).

In order to appreciate fully what John is saying, let's take another brief look at the Gnostics he was refuting. In Gnosticism the highest form of the spiritual life was inward, focused on oneself and one's personal walk with God. In Christianity the focus is outward, toward one's brother. The visible neighbor is the focus of authentic Christian spirituality; the invisible and "spiritual" was the focus of Gnostic spirituality. While it is certainly true that many within the modern charismatic movement give evidence of true love for others, self-sacrifice for their neighbor and authentic Christian spirituality, there seems to be a tendency (at least observed by this author) to focus more on the exciting experiences of tongues, healing, and demon-exorcising at the expense of practical love toward one another on a daily basis.

In the first century the Gnostic felt that the ordinary Christian was beneath him or less than him until he became pneumatic. In Gnostic thinking, love for the neighbor, while emphasized, was not as central as the looking inward. We can see how this focus on experience instead of on others tends to lead to division. Sometimes today we try to justify this division on the basis of seeking others to fellowship with who are "spirit-filled like me." An inability to have fellowship with all genuine believers of the body coupled with a tendency to group into spiritual cliques that have shared the same mystical experience is not evidence of the presence of the Spirit. It is twentieth-century Gnosticism and falls under the apostle's rebuke.

The New Testament writers place their focus on the ethical and the moral as the true evidences of having received the baptism of the Holy Spirit. It may be true that these simple evidences — Christian prayer, understanding of grace, consciousness of God's love, assurance of salvation, concern with practical Christianity, the fruit of the Spirit, and love for other Christians — are not particularly spectacular, but to the New Testament writers they are spiritual.

There is an emphasis on the normal and the practical and the simple in the New Testament that often is lacking in the charismatic movement.

With believers today looking for a validating experience, the appeal of the post-conversion "baptism" is great. The charismatic can say, "I know I have received the Holy Spirit because I have had an experience of speaking in tongues." The New Testament writers were also concerned with a validating evidence of spiritual reality; however, as we have seen, speaking in tongues didn't happen to be on their list!

3

Is the gift of the Holy Spirit received after salvation?

Probably one of the most unique distinctives of the doctrinal teachings of the charismatic movement is their belief that the gift of the Spirit or the fullness of the Spirit is received some time after the believer's initial salvation experience. Salvation, they say, is only the first blessing. After salvation the "full Gospel" needs to be appropriated. The evidence that a man has received the gift of the Spirit is supposed to be that he speaks with other tongues.

However, the New Testament seems to be definite on this point: that the baptism of the Holy Spirit occurs simultaneously with salvation and is the universal work of the Spirit on *all* Christians *at the time they believe*. There are numerous passages of Scripture that substantiate this conclusion.

(1) If a man isn't in the body of Christ he can't be a Christian. Conversely, if he is a Christian, he is in the body of Christ. According to 1 Corinthians 12:13 the baptism with the Holy Spirit is the way in which believers are placed into the body of Christ. Thus, all Christians received the baptism at the time they believed.

(2) 1 Corinthians 12:13 asserts that *all* have been baptized by the Spirit. This "all" included the carnal Christians at Corinth. Thus it is universally true of believers, and the only way that that can be true is if the baptism is something that comes with salvation.

57

(3) "There is one body and one Spirit — just as you were called to one hope when you were called — one Lord, one faith, one baptism; one God and Father of all, who is over all and through all and in all" (Eph. 4:4-6). If not all Christians have the one baptism (the baptism of the Spirit), then all Christians do not have all the other things in the list: one Lord, one God, one faith, and so on. The baptism of the Spirit must be part of salvation and is received at the moment of belief.

(4) Whenever the baptism of the Spirit is mentioned, it is always in the indicative mood in the Greek, and never the imperative mood. This means it is presented as a statement of fact rather than as something we are commanded to seek. If it were important for Christian experience to seek the baptism of the Spirit after salvation, why is it never commanded?

(5) Paul asserts in Galatians 3:26, 27 that to be a son of God, a Christian, means that you have been baptized into Jesus Christ (the baptism of the Spirit). Furthermore, he states that this is true of all: "You are all sons of God through faith in Christ Jesus, for all of you who were united with Christ in baptism have been clothed with Christ." Colossians 2:12 and Romans 6:3 emphasize the same principle.

The epistles clearly teach that the receiving of the Spirit is part and parcel with salvation. Look at Romans 8:9: "...and if anyone does not have the Spirit of Christ, he does not belong to Christ." The Spirit of Christ is the Holy Spirit. To not have the Holy Spirit is to be a non-Christian: "These are the men who divide you, who follow mere natural instincts and do not have the Spirit" (Jude 19).

"But in Acts it says . . ."

Certain passages in the book of Acts definitely teach that in the transitional period between the Old Covenant and the New Covenant there was a receiving of the Holy Spirit that was subsequent to salvation. What are these apparent exceptions and how are they to be explained in the light of the clear teaching of the epistles that the gift of the Spirit is simultaneous with salvation?

Acts 2

Much often is made of the point that the disciples were Christians before Pentecost, although they didn't receive the Spirit until that day, as related in Acts 2. Our charismatic brothers hold that in the same way Christians today are to receive the gift of the Spirit subsequent to the time they believe in Christ.

We have to remember that Acts is a transitional book, spanning the years between the synagogue and the church, from the law to grace, from Old Testament saints to New Testament Christians, and from an exclusively Jewish body of believers to the body of Christ, in which there is neither Jew nor Gentile.

Acts 2 is the fulfillment of an Old Testament promise of an event that was to occur with the advent of the Messiah. This event was the outpouring of the Holy Spirit on Old Testament saints. This occurrence obviously would be after the salvation experience of any Old Testament saint (for example, the disciples). Old Testament saints were those who had heard and believed the promises of God concerning the Messiah, Jesus, before His coming, and were justified by their faith, or trust, in Him. Any who were alive during Jesus' lifetime would have received the Spirit after being saved, because the Spirit was not sent until after Jesus' death.

But once the transition between the Old and the New Covenants had been accomplished, the Spirit was poured out, and He was then available for all who believed in Christ at the point in time when they believed, as the epistles teach. And so it continues today.

Acts 8

Here the case is a little more difficult. The Spirit already has been poured out in Acts 2, yet these believers trusted Christ (Acts 8:12) and were baptized in the name of Jesus and still had not received the gift of the Holy Spirit until Peter and John were sent down to them from Jerusalem and laid hands upon them. This is a clear case of New Testament saints who believed on Christ but did not receive the Spirit until after their salvation. How can we explain it?

Acts 1:8 tells us that as the Spirit was given the apostles were to be witnesses in three successive areas: first Jerusalem and Judea, then Samaria, and finally to the uttermost parts of the earth. This actually is more an ethnic distribution than geographical. The apostles are to be witnesses to the Jews, then the Samaritans, and then the Gentiles.

Drawing on this, we may conveniently outline the book of Acts:

   I. To the Jews: Jerusalem and Judea (Acts 2:1 to 8:4).
   II. To the Samaritans: Samaria (Acts 8:4 to 9:43).
   III. To the Gentiles: the ends of the earth (Acts 10:1 to 28:31).

As the Gospel was preached to each of these three ethnic groups, there was a manifestation of speaking in tongues (though not mentioned in chapter 8, it probably occurred). Tongues served as a sign that the Spirit was being poured out on these different groups into which the ancient Jews divided mankind. The point is this: apparently the Spirit was not poured out on every ethnic group in Acts 2. In Acts 2 He was given only to the Jews. There would be a delay before the Spirit would be poured out on the Samaritans and the Gentiles. This doesn't explain the further delay of the Spirit's arrival in the case of the Samaritans, but it helps to set the context for our second point.

Eyewitness news

One of the major problems in the transitional age was that of getting the Jews in Jerusalem to believe that the kingdom blessings were for Samaritans and Gentiles as well. There was already a Jewish synagogue and a Samaritan place of worship (John 4:20). Both groups claimed to be the true people of God. The Jews considered the Samaritans to be half-breed Jewish-Gentile pagans, and therefore unclean. Any self-respecting Jew would have nothing to do with a Samaritan (John 4:9), let alone a Gentile.

There was real danger that this problem would be perpetrated in the new age in the form of separate Jewish and Samaritan churches. The only way to prevent this was to identify undeniably the experience of the Samaritans with that of the Jews, with the signs accompanying the gift of the Spirit that were witnessed in Jerusalem.

So when Philip preached to the Samaritans and they believed, God delayed the gift of the Spirit until representatives from Jerusalem could arrive. Apparently it was God's purpose that the Holy Spirit was to be imparted through the agency of Peter and John. In that way the signs accompanying the gift to the Samaritans would be witnessed by these two apostles, resulting in positive proof that the experience in Jerusalem at Pentecost was paralleled exactly by the experience of the Samaritans. So any possibility of two different churches would be eliminated.

Acts 10

A similar event occurs in Acts 10 when for the first time the Gospel goes to the Gentiles. Cornelius, a Gentile who lived in the Samaritan city of Caesarea, received the gift of salvation and the sign of speaking in tongues (Acts 10:44–48). This Roman centurion was used by God to teach Peter a lesson: Gentiles were no longer to be considered unclean. This is what the whole context is about (10:15).

This is a further illustration of the problem of the transitional age: how do you get the Jewish Christians to believe that Gentiles are to share in the salvation brought by the Jewish Messiah? In Cornelius's case the Holy Spirit was given simultaneously with the gift of salvation. Why? Because the representative from Jerusalem, Peter, was there to see it. The pattern seems to be that God wants no doubt to exist about the validity of the experiences of these other groups: having a representative of the Jerusalem church there to witness it for the first time accomplishes this.

It is interesting to note that Peter is the agent of the giving of the Holy Spirit to the Jews in Acts 2. And to the Samaritans in Acts 8. And to the Gentiles in Acts 10. It seems to have been God's purpose to impart this gift through the one to whom He had given the keys to the kingdom, the authority to open the kingdom blessings to the Jews, Samaritans, and Gentiles.

"All right," you may be saying, "your line of

evidence does seem plausible, but is there any indication in the text itself that this is the reason for a delayed indwelling?" Yes, there is. Acts 11 alludes to the problems of overcoming the resistance of the Jews to letting the Gentiles into the church. In Acts 11 we have Peter arguing before the Jews in Jerusalem in the same way we have been arguing here. Peter reasons that the experience of Cornelius of speaking in tongues proves that the Gentiles are recipients of exactly the same kingdom blessings as the Jews (Acts 11:15-18). The church at Jerusalem can't argue because Peter was the agent of the giving of the Spirit and he witnessed the same sign manifestations that were given in Jerusalem at Pentecost.

The phenomenon of a delayed indwelling of the Spirit, or baptism of the Spirit, is never repeated in the entire New Testament. To reason from the one event in Acts 8 that this phenomenon is to be the norm of the church age is unwarranted, especially in view of the fact that the doctrinal statements of the epistles are contrary to the charismatic interpretation of Acts 8.

Acts 19

Some charismatic leaders have argued from the King James translation of Acts 19:2 that the receiving of the Holy Spirit is subsequent to salvation: "He said unto them, Have ye received the Holy Spirit since ye believed?..." It is the word "since" that forms the basis for this interpretation. However, "since" is an incorrect translation of the original.[1] A better translation, and the one used

---

[1] "Since ye believed" is an aorist participle. A basic rule of Greek grammar requires the action of an aorist participle to be either simultaneous with or antecedent to the action of the main verb (see H. E. Dana and Julius F. Mantey: *A Manual of the Greek New Testament,* p. 104). The main verb is "received." Therefore, the action of believing is simultaneous with

in the RSV, the ASV, and the New American Standard Bible, would be: "...Have you received the Holy Spirit *when* you believed?..."

As to why Paul should even ask that question, it appears that it is a situation parallel to Acts 2, in which the recipients of the Spirit were Old Testament saints. Verse 3 tells us that these men were disciples of John the Baptist: they were waiting for the Messiah and His kingdom. They simply had not been informed yet that the Messiah had come. This is another of the problems of the transitional period: there were thousands of true believers all over the world at this time who did not even know about Jesus of Nazareth.

The "pattern" of the book of Acts

Frequently the charismatic movement asserts that the pattern for Christian experience now is to be found in the experiences of the early church as recorded in Acts. Just what pattern do we actually find in this book?

What about the 3,000?

We should note first of all that 3,000 people in Acts 2:41 apparently received the Spirit at the time of salvation. Peter says that if a man repents and is baptized, he will receive the gift of the Holy Spirit (2:38). In Acts 10 the Spirit fell upon Cornelius when he believed and before he was baptized (10:44), indicating that baptism is not prerequisite for receiving the Spirit. Therefore, repenting and receiving Christ results in receiving the gift of the Spirit. The 3,000 had repented and had been baptized. Therefore, they must have received the Spirit, but we find no evidence that

---

the action of the receiving of the Holy Spirit. This is an example of the participle of coincident action, as explained by J. H. Moulton in his *Grammar of New Testament Greek*, Vol. I, p. 130.

they spoke in tongues. It is our contention that the experience of the 3,000 is the norm of this age.

There are two groups of believers in Acts 2 who received the gift of the Holy Spirit: the 120 who received the Spirit after being saved, and the 3,000 who received it at the time of their salvation. Why should we pick the experience of the 120 as the norm?

Old vs. new

In every case in the book of Acts in which the Spirit was received subsequent to salvation, those receiving Him were Old Testament believers. The norm for these believers who were alive at the time when the blessings of the new age were being poured out was to receive those blessings after they were saved. The only exception to this is the case of the Samaritans in Acts 8, as we saw earlier.

In Acts 2 the 120 were Old Testament believers. In Acts 10, Cornelius was a Gentile believer from the Old Testament dispensation (10:2, 3) who had not yet entered into the benefits of the new age. In Acts 19 we are dealing with some more Old Testament saints, disciples of John the Baptist.

Three ethnic groups

Tongues occurred only four times, and each time there was a unique situation, in that the Gospel was making its first entrance into the three ethnic groups of Jews, Samaritans, and Gentiles. Each time the sign gifts that authenticated the Gospel were necessary.

Wind and fire

If Acts 2 is going to be the pattern for receiving the gift of the Spirit, then we must include the sound of wind and the appearance of tongues of fire as part of that pattern (2:2). What grounds can we find for taking only one of the three authenticating signs out of the list and making that one the "pattern" sign?

Where's Peter?

If the experience of Acts 8, 10, or 19 is the pattern, then we must insist that an apostle be present.

Seek to speak?

In no case except Acts 2 did the gift of tongues come on someone who was looking for it. So why not pick Acts 10 for our model and say that you should not seek the gift of tongues? Which "pattern" do you choose?

Some or all?

In each case in Acts when the gift of tongues was given it was given to the whole group. In no case did only some of the believers present receive the gift, leaving the others to continue to seek it. So if we are going to maintain that the book of Acts is the "pattern," we have to say that the Spirit must come upon entire groups of believers, with all receiving the gift of tongues.

Apostles and epistles

To sum up, the events of Acts should be interpreted always in view of the doctrine presented in the epistles. We must not make the tragic mistake of teaching the experience of the apostles, but rather we must experience the teaching of the apostles. The experience of the apostles is found in the transitional book of Acts, while the teaching of the apostles is set forth clearly in the epistles, which are our guide for our Christian experience today.

4

Is the gift of tongues for everyone, and should all Christians seek it?

In their enthusiasm for their newfound joy in Christ, many of our Pentecostal brothers and sisters have taught that all Christians should receive the gift of tongues. Out of their love for others, they desire that everyone experience what they have experienced. Unfortunately, this sincerity has led to some frustration and some teaching on spiritual gifts that in my personal opinion strays from the New Testament. The Scriptures seem to be clear on the fact that the gift of tongues was never intended for all believers and is not a sign or evidence of having received the baptism with the Holy Spirit.

To one ... to another

In 1 Corinthians 12:8 we read: "To one there is given through the Spirit the ability to speak with wisdom, to another the ability to speak with knowledge by means of the same spirit"; and 12:9 continues, "to another...to another..." etc. The force of these phrases indicates that all do not have all of the gifts. One person has this gift; another person has that gift.

As who determines?

"All these are the work of one and the same Spirit, and he gives them to each man, just as he determines" (1 Cor. 12:11). The King James Version reads, "dividing to every man severally as he will." The word translated "severally" is the

Greek word *idios*. We get our word "idiot" from it. Paul is saying that the Spirit gives us each our own *peculiar* gift. The word has the idea of "uniquely one's own." Thus everyone has his own unique gifts, which aren't necessarily the same as someone else's gifts.

Note also that these gifts are given as He determines, not as the individual believer determines. The Christian is not to look over the gifts as he would look over the spring coat selection at Sears and say, "I want that one!" He doesn't have that right. The Spirit sovereignly decides. So to seek the gift of tongues actually would be sin: it would be giving orders to God about what He may or may not have sovereignly purposed to do.

"Eye wants to be an ear"

"If the foot should say, 'Because I am not a hand, I do not belong to the body,' it would not for that reason cease to be part of the body" (1 Cor. 12:15). Apparently there was some envy and jealousy going on in Corinth over desire for gifts. Brother Foot wanted to be a hand. Sister Ear felt inferior because she wasn't an eye. The parts of the body listed here represent the various spiritual gifts, or rather, spiritually gifted men. Paul teaches that a believer who has the gift of helps shouldn't desire to have the gift of teaching, or the gift of tongues, or any other gift.

"If the whole body were an eye, where would the sense of hearing be? If the whole body were an ear, where would the sense of smell be?" (1 Cor. 12:17). Paul teaches that God does not intend the whole body to have the same gift. The charismatic movement seems to say that the body should be all "tongue." But it would be sin to start a movement that centers on one gift, i.e., a "tongues movement."

It's interesting that although the gift of helps is also a gift of the Spirit no one seems to have any desire to start a "helps movement." Or what about a "giving movement"? Doesn't it seem strange that the charismatic movement has centered on the more outwardly showy and miraculous gifts and the ones that are the least edifying to others but the most edifying to oneself?

The implied "no"

"Do all have gifts of healing? Do all speak in tongues? Do all interpret?..." (1 Cor. 12:30). We've already seen that the Greek construction here requires a negative answer. All do *not* have the gift of tongues, nor is it God's purpose that the body of Christ be all tongue, or all prophet, or all teacher, or all of any one gift.

Charismatics argue that the gift is for everyone from the following verses:

God's Word or myth?

Mark 16:17 states: "And these signs will accompany those who believe: In my name they will drive out demons; they will speak in new tongues." In all probability this passage should not even be included in the Bible. The two best manuscripts, the Sinaiticus and the Vaticanus, do not include it. The King James Version, which does include it, is based on Greek manuscripts that date from around the tenth century. Sinaiticus and Vaticanus date to the fourth century. Our best evidence is the earliest evidence, and the oldest manuscripts do not include Mark 16:17.

Coveting gifts

"But eagerly desire the greater gifts..." (1 Cor. 12:31). Some say this teaches all believers should seek the gift of tongues. But Scripture goes on:

(1) 1 Corinthians 14:5 indicates that the gift

of prophecy is to be preferred over the gift of tongues: "I would like every one of you to speak in tongues, but I would rather have you prophesy. He who prophesies is greater than one who speaks in tongues. . . ."

Tongues are primarily for use among non-believers, but even in the church and with interpretation they aren't as valuable as prophecy. So if you are going to seek the greater gifts, seek prophecy rather than tongues.

(2) In 1 Corinthians 12:28 the numbers before the gifts indicate that the gifts are listed in order of importance: "And in the church God has appointed first of all apostles, second prophets, third teachers, then workers of miracles, also those having gifts of healing, those able to help others, those with gifts of administration, and finally those speaking in different kinds of tongues." True, any list has something at the top and something at the bottom. But when the thing at the top is specifically designated as "first" and the next as "second" and so on, we would normally conclude that a descending order is intended. So if you are determined to seek a gift, don't seek tongues but one of the greater gifts, one closest to the top of the list.

(3) The Greek verb translated "covet" or "eagerly desire" is not singular but plural, indicating that Paul is exhorting the church as a whole (plural) instead of directing himself to the individuals within it (the singular probably would have been used). He simply is charging the church to pray that God would send them men who have the greater gifts in order that they may be a complete church.

Another view has been put forth by Dr. Earl Radmacher. He recently pointed out that the word translated "covet" could be translated in two ways.[1] The Greek verb *zēloō* is in the second person plural, and can be either a statement of fact (indicative) or a command to obey (imperative). Most of the translations we have choose the command form.

If it were translated as a statement of fact it would read, "You are coveting the showy gifts, but I will show you a better way." Radmacher points out that translators follow two basic rules in making this kind of decision. First, they consider the most common usage. In this case it is much more common to translate the verb as a statement of fact than as a command. Second, they consider the immediate context — what the writer says just before and after the word. In this passage Paul has just argued that the gifts of the Spirit are given sovereignly as God wills, so it seems highly unlikely that he would now reverse himself and exhort believers to do the very thing he has been arguing against (1 Cor. 12:11-18).

Note the contrast in verse 31: "But," Paul says, "I have explained it this way, but you are doing it another way, that is, coveting after gifts."

Perhaps Radmacher is right.

(4) The words "greater gifts" seem to indicate that Paul considered some to be of more importance than others. What is he referring to? If you say that the list intends no descending order, then Paul is making a statement which has nothing in the preceding context to clarify what he means by "greater gifts."

---

[1] Dr. Earl Radmacher in a series of messages given at a Campus Crusade for Christ Leadership Training Institute in Philadelphia in December of 1971. These messages can be purchased by writing to Western Conservative Baptist Theological Seminary, 6444 SW Pinebek Way, Portland, Oregon 97222. Ask for Radmacher's tape series on spiritual gifts. They are excellent!

(5) 1 Corinthians 14:39 seems to explain what Paul meant when he said, "But eagerly desire the greater gift." It reads, "Therefore, my brothers, be eager to prophesy, and do not forbid speaking in tongues."

Command or desire?

"I would like every one of you to speak in tongues" (1 Cor. 14:5). Some have argued that this passage is a command by Paul to speak in tongues.[2] But a closer look reveals:

(1) The Greek verb *thelo* is present indicative active (that's a mouthful but it's important!) and not imperative. It is a statement of personal desire and not a command to be obeyed.

(2) In 1 Corinthians 7:7 Paul says, "I wish that all men were as I am...." He is here expressing his personal desire that all people remain unmarried. He uses the same verb, *thelo*, in the present indicative active. Now obviously that is not his command. But if you take 1 Corinthians 14:6 as a command you must also take 1 Corinthians 7:7 as a command.

(3) All Paul is saying is, "It would be wonderful if you all spoke in tongues, but let's keep this thing in balance." Paul wants all believers to have whatever God wants them to have, but he knows that it is up to the sovereignty of the Spirit, and not our individual seeking. It may be true that a church of believers should seek as a group that God will give them men with the various gifts (1 Cor. 12:31), but it is the sovereign choice of the Spirit as to who will receive those gifts, and no amount of prayer will change it. As 1 Corinthians 12:11 reminds us, "...he gives them to each man, just as he determines."

2 Victor Paul Wierwille, *Receiving the Holy Spirit Today* (New Knoxville, Ohio: The Way, Inc., 1968), p. 182.

5

What is the condition for receiving the Holy Spirit?

My wife, Linda, and I went expectantly to a Pentecostal church in Springfield, Oregon. We were new Christians at the time and very anxious to know more of Christ in our personal experience. We had met some brothers and sisters in the Lord who told of finding a deeper walk with Christ through the "baptism in the Spirit" and speaking in tongues. Their experience of "more" was exactly what we were looking for, so we decided to go to a charismatic meeting.

There we found a lively group of believers expressing their praises to God and speaking in tongues. Linda was a little wary, but I insisted that we give this a thorough examination to see if God had anything for us there. At the end of the service the pastor called for anyone who wanted to receive the gift of the Holy Spirit to come forward. I immediately grabbed Linda's hand and dragged her down front, where about thirty people gathered at the altar rail on their knees. Then the pastor began to explain the conditions necessary to receive the Spirit: he told us that we had to be willing to "go all the way" with Christ, and asked, "Are you totally yielded?" We were instructed to adopt a passive frame of mind and to pray as he laid hands on us for the reception of the baptism in the Holy Spirit. I eagerly followed his instructions and prayed silently. I remember how anxious I was to find out what would happen when he laid his hands on my head:

a jolt of electricity? a fountain of strange words gushing up out of my mouth? an ecstatic meeting with the Lord?

My turn came: nothing happened. Linda's turn: nothing. People next to us began to speak in tongues. Why hadn't it happened to us?

I lingered after the service to pose my question, and the pastor and his wife offered to come to our house to discuss it in detail. Three days later when they came, I was thoroughly introduced to the charismatic understanding of the conditions necessary for receiving the Holy Spirit. We had a very cordial evening until Linda and I began to feel that the conditions the pastor was setting down were so difficult they bordered on the impossible. When we concluded we couldn't accept his doctrine, the pastor and his wife left. And we never did receive the "baptism."

Through reading many charismatic writings and talking with scores of people who have experienced tongues, I find that charismatics generally believe there are two basic conditions for receiving the baptism. Let's put them under the scriptural magnifying glass.

CHARISMATICS SAY...
OBEDIENCE

This first condition has at least three aspects usually found in charismatic teaching.[1]

Separation from all known sin

Key to the charismatic concept is the idea that the Holy Spirit will not enter an unclean vessel. You cannot receive the Spirit with sin in your heart.

---

[1] I am deeply indebted to the writing of Frederick Dale Brunner in his masterpiece of scholarship, *A Theology of the Holy Spirit* (Grand Rapids: Eerdmans, 1970), for alerting me to many of the issues discussed in this chapter.

> The second step in the path that leads into the blessing of being baptized with the Holy Spirit is *renunciation of sin....* A controversy with God about the smallest thing is sufficient to shut one out of the blessing.[2]

Since this seems to lead to the conclusion that a man must be sinless before he can receive the gift of the Holy Spirit, charismatics generally hold a special doctrine of sin. Instead of conceiving of sin as a state (as the Bible does, for example, in Eph. 2:1-3), they tend to define it as a conscious attitude or action. Thus the removal of all known sin even though there is unknown sin in the heart is sufficient to receive the baptism.[3]

This seems confusing: it's necessary for me to live a yielded, pure, and holy life in order to receive the Holy Spirit, but how can I do it? How can a Christian live this life before he has received the full gift of the Spirit, and if he is already living that kind of life, then what does the "baptism" have to offer?

According to the New Testament, it is not the sinless, clean, or worthy who receive the gift of the Spirit. It is the ungodly, unclean, and unworthy who receive Him through their trust in Christ's righteousness.

Consider Romans 4:4, 5 in this connection: "Now when a man works, his wages are not credited to him as a gift, but as an obligation. However, to the man who does not work but trusts God who justifies the wicked, his faith is credited as righteousness."

To say that the Holy Spirit and sin cannot re-

2 R. A. Torrey, *The Person and Work of the Holy Spirit* (Grand Rapids: Zondervan, 1974), pp. 217, 218.
3 Lewi Pethrus, *The Wind Bloweth Where It Listeth: Thoughts and Experiences Concerning the Baptism of the Holy Spirit,* 2nd ed. translator Harry Lindblom (Chicago: Philadelphia Book Concern, 1945), p. 42.

main in the same heart is to contradict Scripture. The Holy Spirit and sin do abide in the same heart unless we're willing to affirm sinlessness, in contradiction to 1 John 1:7-10. Sin remains and we are to struggle to overcome it (Rom. 6:12). To tell someone he first must overcome it before he can receive the Spirit is to put him under a law system of works instead of a grace system of faith. The Gospel of grace does not say that we struggle to get victory over sin in order to fulfill conditions necessary for receiving the Spirit. It says that because we already have received the Spirit we can be victorious over sin.

Prayer

This second aspect of obedience emphasized in charismatic teaching usually is based on Luke 11:13, where our Lord says, "If you then, though you are evil, know how to give good gifts to your children, how much more will your Father in heaven give the Holy Spirit to those who ask him!"

From this it is concluded that prayer is necessary for receiving the Holy Spirit. But — two things: first, this passage is not teaching about conditions of the gift of the Spirit, but about the willingness of the Father to give good gifts to His children. When in John 7:37-39 the conditions for receiving the Holy Spirit are specified, we find that there is one condition only, faith in Christ. To "ask for the Holy Spirit" in Luke 11:13 is the same thing as to "believe in Christ" in John 7:37-39. In the passage in Luke, Jesus is being imprecise about conditions because He is not talking about conditions. In His mind, as in Paul's, to believe in Him resulted in the gift of the Holy Spirit and amounted to the same thing as asking for the Spirit.

Second, Luke 11:13 is describing a pre-pentecostal situation. Men were still under the law until the cross. They were not the recipients of the permanent and universal indwelling of the Holy Spirit that Jesus promised to believers in the new age to be effected by His death on the cross (John 14:16, 17). Asking for the power of the Spirit could have been a legitimate prayer in the Old Testament period, but our Lord makes it clear that in the new age prayer is not a condition for receiving the Spirit. The teaching of the epistles abundantly confirms this.

Emptying or yielding

The third aspect of obedience stressed is total yieldedness:

> Body, soul, and spirit must be yielded. Our physical bodies must be pliable under His power.... Utter and complete baptism in the Holy Spirit ... is reached only when there is a perfect yielding of the entire being to Him and one's tongue is surrendered to the control of the blessed Holy Spirit.[4]

The first two aspects of obedience were more outward; this one is more inward and psychological. We are to adopt a passive state of total emptiness. Certainly there is nothing in the New Testament comparable to this. On the contrary, Paul wants the believer always to be in active control both with his will, "The spirits of prophets are subject to the control of prophets" (1 Cor. 14:32), and with his mind, "I will pray with my spirit, but I will also pray with my mind" (1 Cor. 14:15).

FAITH

According to charismatic teaching, faith is the second major condition for receiving the baptism in the Holy Spirit. There are three aspects of

---

4 Ralph M. Riggs, *The Spirit Himself* (Springfield, Mo.: Gospel Publishing House, 1949), p. 67.

this that need careful definition by our scriptural dictionary.

Faith must be directed toward the Holy Spirit

> As there is a faith toward Christ for salvation, so there is a faith toward the Spirit for power and consecration.[5]

We're told that a believer does not receive the Holy Spirit at salvation because at that time his faith is directed toward Christ, not toward the Holy Spirit.

But the New Testament seems to know of no second faith. Paul says that the gift of the Spirit comes "in Christ Jesus" (Gal. 3:10-14) and is an inseparable part of salvation.

Jesus spoke directly to this when He said, "If a man is thirsty, let him come to me and drink. Whoever believes in me, as the Scripture has said, streams of living water will flow from within him." By this He meant the Spirit whom those who believed in Him were later to receive. Up to that time the Spirit had not been given, since Jesus had not yet been glorified (John 7:37-39).

Faith in Christ resulted in the gift of the Spirit, and not a second faith beyond Christ. The only reason these people had not yet received the Spirit was that He had not yet been given to the church and would not be given until after Jesus had been taken up to heaven. Now that Jesus has ascended, the Spirit has been given and is immediately, personally, and permanently available to all who place their faith in Christ for salvation, and at the time they believe.

Faith must be total

A second reason charismatics give as to why faith in Christ at salvation is inadequate for re

---

[5] Myer Pearlman, *Knowing the Doctrine of the Bible* (Springfield, Mo.: Gospel Publishing House, 1937), p. 316.

78

ceiving the gift of the Holy Spirit is that it is not a total faith:

> As you were justified and regenerated by faith and sanctified by faith, so also you must receive the baptism of the Holy Ghost and fire — the Comforter, by faith. I am supposing that you have yielded to God *at every point....* Are you willing to *go all the way with Christ?*[6]

The ideal of totality is central. Total obedience plus total faith will result in the baptism in the Holy Spirit. The believer is asked to yield at every point and to go all the way with Christ: this is certainly a devout work, but it's not what the New Testament calls faith. The order has been reversed. Instead of the believer depending on God in simple trust to effect a total dedication, he is asked to accomplish this dedication by himself before he is worthy to receive God, i.e., the Holy Spirit.

This requirement for total faith defined as absolute surrender is one of the most heartrending features of charismatic doctrine. When one thinks he is speaking in the language of spiritual devotion, he actually is speaking of the excruciating enslavement of the law. These devotional absolutes call a believer not to grace in Christ but to an anguished search within his heart to find what is not there: absolute yieldedness. This leads to all kinds of introspection and worry as to whether he has "really yielded everything" and so on. Since no believer could ever say yes to that without claiming sinlessness (1 John 1:7-10), guilt complexes and bondage and self-absorption inevitably result. The appeal to interior works of devotion is much more enslaving than an appeal to external works such as church attendance, not drinking,

---

6 Thomas Ball Barratt, *In the Days of the Latter Rain* (London: Simpkin, Marshall, Hamilton, Kent, 1909), pp. 214, 215.

not playing cards or dancing, because it appears to be more "spiritual."

Faith must be alone

Paradoxically, the charismatic movement asserts that faith is completely apart from works:

> Seekers...after the baptism in the Spirit should always remember that this experience is also called "The Gift of the Holy Ghost." Gifts are not earned or won by price or merit. Gifts cannot be forced from the giver. The Holy Spirit is a gracious...God-sent Gift, and we receive Him by faith and by faith alone.[7]

But when the freedom of the gift is always joined to certain preconditions (the three aspects of obedience plus the three aspects of faith) how can it be a free gift? It becomes obvious that this definition of faith must be different from what Christians have traditionally called faith.

If faith is not simple trust but absolute surrender, a person has never exercised faith until he has absolutely surrendered every area of his life to Christ, and until he has experienced the Holy Spirit baptism his faith has been imperfect and therefore not really faith.

> Ordinary Christian faith is the despair of all effort; Pentecostal faith is superhuman effort. And if faith can be defined their way, then Pentecostals can say that it is by faith that one experiences the baptism in the Holy Spirit.[8]

THE BIBLE SAYS...

So what is the New Testament condition for receiving the Holy Spirit? The Bible gives a clear answer: faith. So what's faith?

It will help us first to see what the Bible writers say faith is not. They say God's gift is by faith apart from works (Rom. 3:28; Gal. 2:16), so faith

---

7 Riggs, pp. 105, 106.
8 Frederick Dale Brunner, *A Theology of the Holy Spirit* (Grand Rapids: Eerdmans, 1970), p. 111.

is the opposite of doing something. It is simply receiving a free gift. At its heart charismatic teaching is asking us to do something to receive the Spirit; we are asked to put ourselves back under a law system.

In his time Paul had to deal with two errors concerning works that will shed some light on modern charismatic teaching.

The Galatian problem

The church at Galatia was troubled by a group of people who were trying to tell the believers there how to have the fullness of blessing in their Christian life. They were trying to lead the Galatians to "perfection in Christ" (Gal. 3:3). The Greek word translated "perfect" carried the idea of "to complete, to fulfill, to finish."[9] These teachers wanted to bring the Galatian believers the fullness of blessing in the gift of the Holy Spirit (Gal. 3:14), but the problem lay in the conditions these teachers were laying on the believers. Look at this carefully:

> You foolish Galatians! Who has bewitched you? Before your very eyes Jesus Christ was clearly portrayed as crucified. I would like to learn just one thing from you: Did you receive the Spirit by observing the law, or by believing what you heard? (Gal. 3:1, 2).

Notice the absolute distinction Paul draws between receiving the gift of the Holy Spirit through something we do (by works of the law) or by simple trust (believing what you heard). The gift either is received freely or earned by devout effort but not both. He continues: "Are you so foolish? After beginning with the Spirit, are you now trying to attain perfection by human effort?" (3:3).

The teachers were saying that there was another

---

[9] Walter Bauer, *A Greek-English Lexicon of the New Testament*, translated by William F. Arndt and F. Wilbur Gingrich (Grand Rapids: Zondervan, 1957), p. 302.

Gospel, a full Gospel, that would bring the Spirit to them in completion, fullness, or perfection. The simple message of salvation in Christ was only a beginning, they said. They acknowledged that faith was the first step, but encouraged devout effort as a supplement to achieve the fullness of God's blessing. The thing that made them so bewitching was that their message appealed to people's needs, seemed to be based on the Bible, and sounded spiritual. They deceived even the elect, who couldn't see how these teachers could not be of God: they appealed to such high, "spiritual" motives!

For Paul, faith was the only condition for the fullness of salvation: "Does God give you his Spirit and work miracles among you because you observe the law, or because you believe what you have heard?" (3:5).

Whatever faith is, it doesn't involve human effort, however devout, however sincere, however important *as a result of faith*. It is faith alone or it is not New Testament faith. It is at this point that charismatic doctrine falls under the apostle's condemnation.

The Galatian heresy had a "both-and" appeal but note Paul's final summation: "He redeemed us in order that the blessing given to Abraham might come to the Gentiles through Christ Jesus so that *by faith* we might receive the promise of the Spirit" (3:14).

The Colossian problem

Like the Galatians, the Colossians were being troubled with false teachers concerned with introducing them into the "fullness" of their salvation. The message these teachers had for the Colossians is the message the charismatics have for believers

82

today: a "deeper relationship," "more," a "full gospel." The Colossians were being taught that the fullness of blessing lay in uniting with spirit beings "beyond Christ." Having Christ was good, they were told, but more was needed to possess a "full salvation." While charismatics differ from the Colossian teachers in not locating the source of the "more" in spirit beings, they are saying that the source comes from beyond Christ, in this case, from the Holy Spirit.

Notice how Paul countered the first-century teaching:

> For God was pleased to have all his fullness dwell in him, and through him to reconcile to himself all things, whether things on earth or things in heaven, by making peace through his blood, shed on the cross (Col. 1:19, 20).

The Colossians were being tempted to look for "fullness" beyond Christ. Paul stresses that they already have this fullness *because they are in Christ*. He says the same thing in Ephesians:

> Praise be to the God and Father of our Lord Jesus Christ, who has blessed us in the heavenly realms with every spiritual blessing in Christ (Eph. 1:3).

Is it logically possible to look for more once you have received *every* spiritual blessing?

> For in Christ all the fullness of the Deity lives in bodily form, and you have this fullness in Christ, who is the head over every power and authority (Col. 2:9, 10).

The believer already has everything. Absolutely nothing can be added. In the first century any teaching of a "fullness beyond Christ" was called heresy. Should it be called less in the twentieth? So we see that in both Galatia and in Colosse believers were being troubled by teachers who taught some of the same things as modern Pentecostalism. They both were troubling believers about the "full Gospel." In Galatia they were saying that the fullness of blessing came by devout human effort beyond faith. In Colosse, they were saying that the fullness of blessing resided beyond the initial salvation in Christ.

So What?
(How does this affect me?)

All this might seem rather theological (and it is!), but it has significant lessons for us in our walk with Christ today.

If I ignore it will it go away?

When the Galatian teachers came offering "more" through devout effort, Paul didn't dismiss it with a smile. He said:

> Evidently some people are throwing you into confusion and are trying to pervert the gospel of Christ. But even if we or an angel from heaven should preach a gospel other than the one we preached to you, let him be eternally condemned (Gal. 1:7, 8).

Paul obviously considered this heresy a serious threat to the Gospel of grace and to the body of believers. I'd like to suggest two reasons why believers today should not consider the teaching of the charismatic movement a harmless variation.

A special focus often becomes a substitute

It seems basic to the nature of man that in matters of religion a special focus often becomes a substitute for the main issue. Over and over in church history, whenever a group began to emphasize one particular aspect of biblical truth instead of the grace of God, that aspect became a substitute for the grace of God. This happens because the things that mark one group as unique tend to become more defined as people inquire how that group differs from others. In charismatic groups there is an observed (at least by this author) tendency to place an emphasis on the miraculous gifts at the expense of the grace of God. Speaking in tongues, healings, and demon exorcisms are more important to many within this movement than speaking of salvation in Christ. Their burden is often to introduce others into the Holy Spirit baptism rather than to introduce the lost into the grace of God.

This was illustrated to me forcefully several weeks ago while attending a meeting featuring a well-known faith healer in Pittsburg. After the service I talked to several people, trying to gather information as to why they were there. My first question was, "When did you come to know Christ personally?" All of them began to relate to me various healings they had seen or experienced. I asked for their definition of the Gospel. They defined it as more faith healings, and were terribly unclear and confused. Interestingly enough, when asked how they were going to get to heaven, all of them replied that they would make it on the basis of their sincerity and good works.

The law system of the Galatian "charismatics" already had come to dominate their thinking. Their special focus had become a substitute for the Gospel.

But an illustration like this can be unfair. To argue from the abuses of a few that the whole movement is wrong is unjustified. I have many friends within the charismatic movement who decidedly have not let their tongues speaking get out of focus. For them the issue is the Gospel; tongues speaking is a secondary and incidental "plus" to them, and they wouldn't dream of making it an issue with anyone else. They are as against these abuses as the New Testament is.

But it's still true that, as shown through history, a special focus often does become a substitute, and that has happened in the lives of thousands within the modern charismatic movement. What I'm saying is that the abuse follows *logically* from the theology. For the thousands who have not abused the gift, I suggest that it is not because of their theology but in spite of it. They have developed a real and genuine walk with Christ that brings the needed balance and overrides the unbiblical viewpoint on tongues.

A law system leads to guilt

Approaching a believer with this language of devotion — "going all the way with Christ," "yielded at every point," "are you sure," "have you trusted Him fully" — places a burden of introspection upon the child of God that never was intended by the New Testament. Every believer in Christ would do well to examine his life and look inward, but not in order to receive "more" from God. Paul didn't ask believers to look inward and yield at every point to receive the Spirit, but he did ask them to do this to experience practically the fruits of the Spirit which already had come to indwell them.

In the former case, the believer would be yielding to get something from God. In the latter, he yields because he already has been given something. The former is law and the latter is grace. The former springs from guilt and the latter from love. The former is a "have to" and the latter is a "want to." The difference lies in the motivation.

I remember as a new Christian eagerly reading the writings of the "victorious life" teachers who stressed the same kind of thing (though not charismatics). I forced myself to examine every motive, every attitude. I could always find something wrong and so was never sure I had "gone all the way" and was "totally yielded at every point." So I tried harder to be more yielded so that I could receive *by faith* the fullness of my salvation. Ironic? Yes, but true of many believers.

This fullness never "arrived" because I already had it. God wanted me to simply believe that I already possessed all blessing He could give me, including the "more" I was so ardently seeking. As I realized this, I began to simply believe and to appropriate it. Blessings began to unfold in my life, and I was released from the agony of guilt caused by introspection.

"In the same way, count yourselves dead to sin but alive to God in Christ Jesus" (Rom. 6:11). Count it true and it becomes your experience. Simple trust. Believe that it's yours and it is. No striving, no introspection. It doesn't sound as "spiritual" and it's not too spectacular, but it works! It brings joy, peace, and the exciting adventure of knowing the abundant life in Christ.

An aged silver miner had spent all his life searching for silver in the mountains of the Old West. He had become so obsessed with his search that his wife and children had left him. When he died, the handful of people who came to bury him found in his possessions a note instructing them to bury him under his cabin. As the spadesful of earth were turned over a lustrous gray material began to appear. It was the famous Comstock Silver Vein, the richest in California history. That miner had been a billionaire all his life, but he had never claimed his wealth.

Likewise, many believers are spiritual billionaires but never claim the blessings God has for them. Every person who is in Christ has everything God can ever give him. The question is, "Will you claim God's promises by faith and begin living them in your daily walk?" Stop clamoring and start claiming!

6

Did the gift of tongues pass from the church?

A few days ago as I was driving home from an appointment I tuned in on a local Christian radio station. A talk show was on, and the guest that day was a well-known entertainer who had received Christ a short time before and had subsequently spoken in tongues. The interviewer, obviously trying to stir up a little controversy to stimulate call-ins, raised the question of the cessation of the gift. His guest's response was that there was "not one verse in the entire Bible that specifically says that tongues passed from the church." For him that settled the issue.

But for many Christians it doesn't, and with good reason. There are many doctrines in the Bible that have no specific verses to support them. These doctrines are established inductively from a number of passages. For example, there is not one verse in the entire Bible that specifically teaches the Trinity, yet the biblical evidence for the Trinity is so overwhelming that it has never been doubted. There is not one verse that states that Jesus was God-man, but there are scores of passages that teach He was God and scores more that teach He was man. So scholars conclude He was God-man. It's plain that having to cite a specific reference or verse to support a particular teaching is wholly foreign to Christian theology. From the beginning, theologians have avoided basing doctrine on single verses anyway.

Rather, the totality of Scripture must be taken into account.

So when I speak of what I personally consider to be "overwhelming evidence" that the gift of tongues ceased, I am talking about an induction based on the views of the early church and the whole of biblical revelation rather than specific verses.

What about 1 Corinthians 13:8, 9?

There is one passage that has come into the discussion frequently:

> But where there are prophecies, they will cease; where there are tongues, they will be stilled; where there is knowledge, it will pass away. For we know in part and we prophesy in part, but when perfection comes, the imperfect disappears (1 Cor. 13:8, 9).

What is this "perfection"? Some believe that it refers to the closing of the canon, the completion of the Bible when John wrote the book of Revelation in about A.D. 90. If that is true we have a verse that specifically says tongues will pass by the end of the first century.

Others believe that "perfection" refers to the second coming of Christ. In that case, the verse doesn't teach that tongues have already disappeared. But whatever we believe here actually has no bearing on the question of whether or not tongues have passed from the church: this conviction is based on other Scriptures.

A good friend of mine, Hal Lindsey, says in his excellent book, *Satan Is Alive and Well on Planet Earth:*

> I had previously believed that all of the sign gifts such as healing, miracles, tongues, and prophecies ceased as bona fide gifts of the Spirit about the end of the first century, just after the New Testament was completed. The Scripture usually cited to prove this thesis is 1 Corinthians 13:8-12....
>
> ... This is admittedly a difficult passage of Scrip-

ture, but I have come to believe that the "perfect" refers to a condition which will be true of us when Christ returns. . . . Therefore it is my opinion that this passage alone is not enough to warrant the forbiddance of tongues today.[1]

This statement could lead some to think that the case for the cessation of the gift is based solely on the Corinthians passage, and that since that passage is disputable we can't build a good case for cessation. But historically 1 Corinthians 13:8, 9 never played a part in the view of the Christian church that tongues ceased in the first centuries: there are at least a hundred other passages that lead us to this conclusion.

In the following pages I would like to suggest fourteen arguments from the Bible that convincingly establish that the gift of tongues was only a temporary phenomenon, limited to the first century.

A word about miracles

Speaking in tongues is one of God's many kinds of miracles. Some charismatic brethren say that if we don't believe God still gives the gift of tongues we aren't believing Him for His other miracles either. How about it? If we say God no longer gives the gift of tongues, does this mean that we think God no longer works miracles?

What about answers to prayer? Our prayer life is built on the basic assumption that there is a definite possibility that God will supernaturally intervene and give a specific answer. If that's not a possibility, if miracles have ceased, then aren't our prayers utter foolishness?

Or what about miraculous healings? We all know someone, possibly ourself, who has been healed in a supernatural way that modern medi

[1] Hal Lindsey, *Satan Is Alive and Well on Planet Earth* (Grand Rapids: Zondervan, 1972), pp. 136, 137.

cine can't explain. God does work miracles today, as Scripture and experience abundantly confirm. How then can we say that one kind of miracle, tongues, has ceased?

Two kinds of miracles

To answer that question, it will be helpful to define the two kinds of biblical miracles.[2]

Category one

God acts through the laws of nature in such a way that the end product is our realization, "I know that God was at work." When Satan was allowed by God to test Job (Job 1:12) many "miraculous" things happened to Job which were simply the product of Satan's working through natural laws. When Job's servants reported that the fire of God had fallen on Job's sheep and servants and killed them (1:16), what undoubtedly happened was that a lightning storm destroyed the barn.

In the same way, when Paul speaks of the Father giving comfort (2 Cor. 1:4), are we to look for some miraculous and mystical inner peace that the Father will pour out on us? Possibly, but probably not. Further on in the same book Paul says that comfort came to him through purely natural means, the coming of Titus and his report of the love the Corinthians had for Paul (2 Cor. 7:7).

The Bible says God will lead us (Prov. 3:5, 6). Is this through a vision, a dream, or some mystical insight? The book of Proverbs goes on to show how God leads, at least in some cases, through a multitude of counselors (Prov. 11:14). In these examples God leads through a purely natural law.

We find Paul making decisions concerning the

---

2 Helmut Thielicke, *Man in God's World* (New York: Harper and Row, 1963), pp. 100-104.

will of God by examining the circumstances (1 Cor. 16:8, 9). He prayed that God would send him to Rome to preach the Gospel (Rom. 1:10). And the prayer was answered, not by God miraculously transporting Paul there, but through a series of natural causes: he was arrested and eventually sent to Rome for trial.

In all of the above workings of God, we truly have miracles. But it was God acting through natural laws in such a way that the product convinced the believers involved that God was at work.

Helmut Thielicke gives a beautiful illustration of this from his own experience.[3] Some years ago he lay paralyzed with medical science unable to help him. He had only a few months to live. Then just as his body was about to fail, a new drug was discovered that saved his life. What happened? He was convinced, and I agree, that God had intervened. Yet it happened quite naturally: from a human viewpoint it was only a matter of two chains of events happening to cross each other at a certain point in time. On the one hand his illness was advancing relentlessly to its terminal point, and somewhere else in Germany a medical researcher who knew nothing about Thielicke was feverishly at work in his laboratory developing a cure for that very disease. And at the last moment, the two series of events intersected.

There was nothing overtly miraculous or supernatural about this at all, but it was clearly the miracle of answered prayer that saved Thielicke's life. He could only say, "The Lord has done this." God arranged those events to meet at that specific point. This kind of miracle definitely occurs today.

Category two

This type of miracle consists of violations of the

3 Ibid., pp. 101, 102.

laws of nature. Natural law is suspended and God supernaturally intervenes. The Bible contains many examples of this. When Jesus stilled the storm (Mark 4:35-41) the laws of nature were set aside and the supernatural took over. The same is true in Daniel's deliverance out of the lions' den (Dan. 6) and the parting of the Red Sea (Exod. 14).

This category really has three separate subdivisions:

1) Periods of revelation

First there are miracles related to special periods of revelation, such as the time of Moses and Joshua, of Elijah and Elisha, and of Christ and the apostles. During these periods this kind of miracle was the norm: they were God's most common way of operating through His messengers and constituted signs. But God's working in this way was always temporary, as we will see.

2) The miracle gifts

Second, we have the miracles related to the spiritual gifts of the first century. It is my personal belief that these, too, were temporary; they were all specifically related to the nation of Israel and the foundation of the church. More on this later.

3) Exceptions

The Bible speaks of direct interventions by God that were not related to either a special era of revelation nor to the spiritual gifts. These are the exception and not the norm. Examples would be Gideon's fleece (Judges 6), Samson's strength (Judges 13-16), and Daniel's dream interpretations and escapes from the heathen leaders of Babylon and Persia (Dan. 1-6). These miracles are rare and few in comparison with those clustered around the prophetic eras and the spiritual gifts.

It is my belief that the Bible teaches that Category One miracles and the third kind of Category Two miracles continue today, but that they are exceptional and not God's ordinary way of working. The charismatic movement asserts that what was the norm of God's operation in the first century is also His norm in the twentieth. In contrast, the Bible teaches that what was the norm then is the exception today.

We are to look for God on occasion to miraculously intervene in answer to prayer. We are to look for His miraculous leading and comfort and providential care. But it will most often come through natural law; we are not to look for miraculous direct interventions (Category Two) as a way of life. We'll see that these are things that God has promised as part of the kingdom reign when Christ returns.

In the following five chapters I will detail the biblical evidence for the cessation of the gift of tongues in the first century. Although there are fourteen lines of evidence, I find it convenient to group them under five different categories. There are factors relating to God's covenant relationship with Israel; factors relating to the foundation period of the church; factors relating to the closing of the canon; factors relating to the authentication of Christ and His apostles; and finally, factors relating to the historical cessation of the gift of tongues as observed by the book of Acts and the leading church historians.

7

Factors relating to God's covenant relationship to Israel

In the opening chapter of this book, I tried to show that the gift of tongues had a special function in the first century of being a sign of judgment against the nation of Israel. A factor that frequently is overlooked in discussions of the miraculous gifts and of tongues in particular is the intimate connection these gifts and miracles had with God's promises to that nation.

In the Old Testament God made a covenant with that nation, i.e., He made a promise. He promised the nation that one day they would be the focus of a global kingdom of God on planet earth. The New Testament writers inform us that this kingdom will be established with the second coming of Christ. Yet in a real sense the history of the Old Testament and of the Bible in general is the history of the "breaking in" of that kingdom. Periodically, God's kingdom irrupts, or breaks through into this world. Since miracles are part of everyday life in this kingdom, the irruptions of this kingdom always are accompanied by miraculous manifestations. At the second coming of Christ, the kingdom will break in completely and finally be established on planet earth. These "irruptions" are evidences that God is moving to fulfill His promise to Israel. There are three factors connected with this promise that imply the temporary nature of the gift of tongues.

THE PATTERN OF THE BIBLE MIRACLES

Many people get the idea that the Bible is an account of continuous miracles from Genesis to Revelation. Actually, miracles in the Bible are the exception, and always are connected with God fulfilling His promise to the Jews. There are only three major outbreaks of miracles in the Scriptures.

Moses and Joshua (1441-1370 B.C.)

God was moving to deliver His people out of Egypt. Moses' credentials were authenticated by the miracles he performed: Exodus 4:1-5 says these miracles proved that Moses was God's deliverer. Also, new revelation was being given: the law, the tabernacle, and the prophecies of Israel's future (Deut. 28-30). Miracles were needed to authenticate Moses and his message, and Joshua and his authority. After the people came out of Egypt and conquered Canaan, the miracles ceased.

Elijah and Elisha (870-785 B.C.)

The worship of Baal had become a serious threat to Israel's existence as a theocratic nation. In the midst of this situation, God raised up Elijah and Elisha to promote revival to stem the time of moral declension and to call the nation to repentance. Again, miracles were needed to prove that these men were from God (1 Kings 18:20-40). Once these prophets had been authenticated and God's unique message through them delivered, the miracles ceased.

Christ and the apostles (A.D. 28-70)

The final cluster of sign manifestations in the Bible centers around the first coming of Christ. God had become a man. Obviously, proof was needed to validate that claim! John tells us that these miracles were a source of proof (John 20:30-31). Paul tells us that the miracles of the apostle were related to proving their authority (2 Cor. 12:12; 1 Cor. 14:22).

Note that every time there was a cluster of sign manifestations, there were two things involved: new revelation, and a man (or men) of God whose credentials as the bearer(s) of that revelation needed to be verified. Furthermore, the miracles never broke out *before* the messenger and his revelation had arrived but only *afterward*. Thus, we are not to expect any miracles before the second coming of Christ but only afterward.

One of the greatest scholars on the subject of miracles, Richard Trench, wrote,

> We do not find the miracles sown broadcast over the whole Old Testament history, but they all cluster around a very few eminent persons, and have reference to certain great epochs and crises of the kingdom of God.[1]

The following time line illustrates the biblical pattern of miracles.

Moses and Joshua		Elijah and Elisha		Christ and Apostles	
1 B.C.	1370 B.C.	870	785	A.D. 28	A.D. 90
	500 years		814 years		
70 years		70 years		70 years	

This shows that the sign manifestations always were temporary, lasting about seventy years each time they appeared. Furthermore, there were gaps between them in which God was silent. This helps explain the silence of God over the last nineteen centuries and the disappearance of the miraculous gifts at the end of the first century.

We should at the same time remember that be-

---

1 Richard Chenevix Trench, *Notes on the Miracles and Parables of Our Lord* (Westwood: Fleming H. Revell Co., 1953), pp. 49, 50.

tween these great periods of sign manifestations there were scattered miracles for specific purposes. But no one would have argued from those few miracles that that was God's *normal* operation for that time. Likewise, no one doubts that the Lord Jesus Christ is performing miracles today. The question is whether this is the norm. The charismatic movement says that it should be and the Bible says it shouldn't!

A Taste of the Coming Age

A careful reading of the ancient prophecies leaves one with the definite impression that the miraculous as a way of life was characteristic of the life of the believer only during the kingdom when Christ returns. When these miracles broke through into everyday life, they were simply irruptions of God's kingdom. Since they were intimately related with God's kingdom, and since we are not yet in that kingdom, the miracles of the first century, including tongues, must be viewed as a temporary irruption of that kingdom and not a norm for this non-kingdom age. Therefore, the charismatic error is not so much that they argue for the continuance of gifts that have ceased, but that they claim an experience of gifts that have to be introduced. It is not that they are too late, but, according to the Bible, they are too early!

Perhaps a good way to outline this thought is to consider the following syllogism:

Major premise: The miraculous is to be a way of life only in the future kingdom when Christ returns.

Minor premise: We are not yet in that future kingdom.

Conclusion: The miraculous is not the norm of daily life today. Consequently

the gifts of the first century must
be viewed as temporary "breakthroughs" of that kingdom.

The conclusion of any syllogism is only as valid
as its premise. The minor premise will appear
obvious to most, hence it is to the major premise
that I will direct my attention. Does the Bible
associate the miracles only with the kingdom of
God?

The Old Testament prophecies

According to the ancient prophets, God will
one day establish a global kingdom in fulfillment
of His promise to David (1 Chron. 17:11-15; Isa.
2:1-5; 9:6, 7; Amos 9:11-15). The miraculous will
be the common daily experiences of believers in
this kingdom. Men will live hundreds of years (Isa.
65:20). Wolves and lambs will feed together (Isa.
65:25). Furthermore, it will be an unparalleled
age of the fullness of the Spirit (Isa. 32:15; 41:1;
44:3; 59:19, 21; 61:1; Jer. 31:33; Ezek. 36:27;
37:14).

Let's look at one of the Old Testament passages
in which this kingdom is predicted (Isa. 35:1-6).

> The wilderness and the desert will be glad and the
> Arabah will rejoice and blossom; It will blossom
> profusely.

This refers to an arid region today. In the kingdom it will become a fertile plain.

> Then the eyes of the blind will be opened and the
> ears of the deaf will be unstopped. Then the lame
> will leap like a deer, And the tongue of the dumb
> will shout for joy.

Note that one of the characteristics of the kingdom would be divine healing. These passages (and
scores of others could be cited), show that the
prophets expected that the kingdom of God on
earth would be a time of unusual miraculous ac-

tivity. It would become the norm of the believer's experience.

The New Testament writers

Not only did the Old Testament prophets describe the future kingdom as a time of miracles, but the New Testament writers believed that the miracles performed by Christ and the apostles were connected with the establishment of that kingdom. They thought the "coming age" had come. The reign of Israel was about to begin (cf. Acts 1:6). Since these miracles, in their eyes, were connected only with the establishment of God's kingdom reign on earth, we conclude that they would not have expected them to continue unless God's kingdom was indeed established. However, that kingdom wasn't established. Hence the miracles associated with its temporary breakthrough did not continue because they were never anticipated as part of the period of history when the kingdom had not yet been established.

In proof of this assertion that the New Testament writers viewed the miracles they were seeing as uniquely related to the future kingdom in agreement with the Old Testament prophets, consider two passages.

The question of John the Baptist

After John had been imprisoned, he began to wonder whether or not Jesus was the Messiah after all. He expected Israel's kingdom to be established immediately but Jesus didn't seem to be following that program. So John sent some messengers to Jesus to ask Him whether or not He was in fact the promised Messiah who would establish God's kingdom on earth. They said,

> Are you the one who was to come, or should we expect someone else?

Jesus replies by quoting the passage from Isaiah 35:1-6 that we cited above.

> Jesus replied, "Go back and report to John what you hear and see: The blind receive sight, the lame walk, those who have leprosy are cured, the deaf hear, the dead are raised, and the good news is preached to the poor" (Matt. 11:4, 5).

This passage is very important. Here Jesus, by quoting the Old Testament, says that the miracles He was performing were the miracles of the kingdom of God. The kingdom of God was making another breakthrough in the person of the King. These miracles, according to Jesus, are miracles associated with the predicted kingdom of God and not with the present age. Had the kingdom of God been established, of course the miracles associated with it would have continued. And when the kingdom of God is established in the "coming age" at the second coming of Christ, miracles will once again be part of the daily life of believers.

The sermon of Peter

In Acts 2 Peter connects the miracles of the new age and the tongues experience in particular with the coming kingdom of God. Peter, and most of the early believers, expected that the predicted reign of Jesus would be established in their lifetime. When the Holy Spirit descended upon them in this chapter and they spoke in tongues, it was another breakthrough of the miraculous kingdom. Peter clearly testified that in his mind the tongues of Acts 2 were a breakthrough of the kingdom and were associated with that kingdom. He does this by quoting an Old Testament passage which predicted a global outpouring of the Spirit upon all men during God's global kingdom on earth. The passage he cites is from the book of Joel. Let's look at the context of Joel 2 carefully.

In verses 21-27 Joel describes the many blessings

that Israel will experience in the future kingdom after being delivered from the invading army to the North (cf. vv. 12-20). These blessings are summed up in verse 27:

> Thus you will know that I am in the midst of Israel,
> And that I am the Lord your God
> And there is no other;
> And My people will never be put to shame.

Here Joel describes what it will be like in a future day when the Jewish people have been regathered into their ancient land and established in their kingdom. The nation has returned to faith in God, they know He is in their midst and His people will never again be put to shame!

Now consider verse 28:

> And it will come about *after this*
> That I will pour out My Spirit on all mankind.

After what? After the events of verses 21-27, i.e., after Israel is in her land acknowledging the God of her fathers once again. Thus, the outpouring of God's Spirit was to occur after Israel was established in her kingdom and not before. Many Pentecostals are prone to quote this passage as proof that the present-day tongues phenomenon is a sign of the second coming of Christ. Yet a careful examination of the context clearly shows that Joel predicted no such pre-second advent sign. The outpouring that Joel talks about occurs after Jesus returns and not before. Israel today is in unbelief. Many are atheists. They have not returned to the God of their Fathers and therefore this passage has no bearing on the prophetic situation today.

If the Joel prediction applies to the time period after the Second Coming, why did Peter seemingly quote it as being fulfilled by the events at Pentecost? This is admittedly a difficult question and various interpretations have been given. I personally feel that Peter was citing this passage not to emphasize that it was being fulfilled at Pentecost but to answer the charge of drunkenness. The enthusiasm of the disciples after experiencing the power of the Spirit was interpreted as drunkenness by the religious leaders. Peter answers by citing Joel 2. In effect he is saying, "How can you call this enthusiasm drunkenness? Our own Bible anticipates such an exhilarating experience in the book of Joel. What you are seeing here at Pentecost is an illustration of what Joel said would happen in the kingdom reign. If such enthusiasm is O.K. then, why do you rebuke it now?" Notice Peter's words carefully,

> These men are not drunk, as you suppose. It's only nine in the morning! No, this is what was spoken by the prophet Joel:
> "In the last days, God says,
>   I will pour out my Spirit on all people.
> Your sons and daughters will prophesy,
>   your young men will see visions,
>   and your old men will dream dreams.
> Even on my servants, both men and women,
>   I will pour out my Spirit in those days,
>   and they will prophesy.
> And I will show wonders in the heaven above
>   and signs on the earth below,
>   blood and fire and billows of smoke.
> The sun will be turned to darkness
>   and the moon become as blood
>   before the coming of the great and glorious
>   day of the Lord.
> And everyone who calls on the name of the
>   Lord will be saved" (Acts 2:15-21).

Peter says that the events of Acts 2 are *what* Joel spoke of but not necessarily the fulfillment of what Joel spoke of! He couldn't have intended that meaning because most of the things Peter quotes never happened (e.g., wonders in the sky, Spirit poured out on *all* mankind, sun turned to darkness, moon turned to blood). Thus, Peter is saying that the tongues experience in Acts 2 is a specimen of the miraculous era of the kingdom that Joel talked about. We conclude then by affirming that the tongues phenomenon of Acts 2 was a breakthrough of the kingdom. It was a specimen of what it will be like in the "coming age." Had that kingdom been established as Peter and the other apostles eagerly hoped it would be, the tongues phenomenon and the other miracles would have continued. However, since the kingdom was not established, and since the miraculous gifts are associated only with the miracles of the kingdom era, we conclude that Peter would not have expected these gifts to remain in the church apart from the full breakthrough of the kingdom on earth.

Why tongues if no kingdom?

Because the kingdom was not established in the first century, the New Testament writers began to view the miracles of the first century not as a continuing experience but as a guarantee of the future coming of the kingdom of God. They were a foretaste of what it will be like when Jesus returns. Let's look at a crucial passage in Hebrews 6:5. The writer speaks of believers who,

> . . . have tasted the goodness of the word of God and the powers of the coming age.

Notice that the "powers" the first-century believers experienced are specified as something that is to be characteristic of the "coming age" (the future kingdom), and are not characteristic of the present age. The writer says that their relation to this present age is that they are a "taste" of "glory divine."

The kingdom had been offered to Israel (Mark 1:15) and rejected. But the lightning flashes witnessed by the men of the first century gave them assurance that one day the reign of God would be established on earth. Since these breakthroughs of the kingdom are always connected in prophecy and in the New Testament with the establishment of Israel's kingdom, when Israel rejects truth, miracles cease. When Israel accepts, at the Second Coming, the miracles will begin once again.

One of the greatest biblical scholars of the nineteenth century, George N. H. Peters, put it this way,

> The Baptism of Pentecost is a pledge of fulfillment in the future, evidencing what the Holy Ghost will yet perform in the coming age.[2]

Helmut Thielicke, the brilliant German theologian, holds the same view. He considers the miracles of the first century as "the lightning on the horizon of the Kingdom of God."

> And these individual signs the New Testament says are the lightning of the Kingdom of God on the horizon, lightning that proclaims the day, the reign of God. And in that kingdom that still stands beyond the horizon and seeks to come to us, guilt and suffering will cease, and even death will be no more. So when things grow hard for us, when the dark descends upon us, when sore fate comes down upon our life, when we no longer know how we shall get through the coming night and the following day, then we are to look to this kingdom, which is already making itself known in the lightning flashes of Jesus' miracles.[3]

In conclusion . . .

In summary, then, let's suggest two basic reasons why we must consider the gift of tongues and the other miracles as a temporary phenomenon related to the first century.

First of all, since the prophecies say these signs and wonders are related to the era in which Israel is in belief in her kingdom, as long as the Jewish

---

2 George N. H. Peters, *The Theocratic Kingdom* (Grand Rapids: Kregel, 1972), reprint of original edition in three volumes published in 1884. Volume 3, p. 66.

3 Helmut Thielicke, *Man in God's World* (New York: Harper and Row, 1963), p. 112.

nation remains in unbelief the miracles will not be operative. God's judgment on Israel was consummated in A.D. 70 and hence we should expect that the signs and wonders associated with Israel's kingdom would cease by then also. To have continued the working of the signs during the past 1900 years of church history when Israel has remained outside the land and in unbelief would have contradicted the prophets who said that these signs were associated with the restoration of that nation in the kingdom of the Messiah. Israel's presence in the land today has no bearing on this question. The prophecies refer to a restored Israel trusting in the "pierced one" (Zech. 12:10), the Lord Jesus Christ. When God once again moves to fulfill His covenant promise to Israel in the kingdom, these miraculous powers once again will become the daily experience of believers. The first-century experience, however, was simply a temporary foretaste, a guarantee of the joys of the coming age.

Second, if these signs and powers are for the present age, then we must "water down" the Old Testament predictions and assume a kind of imperfect fulfillment instead of a full, literal, and glorious fulfillment which the plain reading of the ancient prophecies demands.

THE SIGN OF TONGUES IS NO LONGER NEEDED

The third factor relating to the cessation of the gift of tongues with God's covenant promise to Israel involves the sign nature of the gift. If the gift of tongues was primarily a judicial sign against Jewish unbelief as a nation, then the sign significance of the gift ended with the destruction of Jerusalem in A.D. 70. Jesus viewed the fall of Jerusalem as the judgment of God for Jewish nation unbelief. Since the judgment has been executed

106

the gift that was uniquely for a sign of that judgment is no longer needed. In two parables Jesus says the destruction of Jerusalem would be evidence of God's judgment.

> "He will bring those wretches to a wretched end," they replied, "and he will rent the vineyard to other tenants, who will give him his share of the crop at harvest time" (Matt. 21:41).

> The king was enraged. He sent his army and destroyed those murderers and burned their city (Matt. 22:7).

Israel's day of favor in God's grace was coming to an end rapidly. The second passage seems to be a reference to the armies of Titus, pictured in the parable as the armies of God, and in judgment they *were* the armies of God. God's offer of the kingdom had been rejected, and Israel was judged: the priesthood was destroyed, the sacrifices abolished, the temple torn down, and the people dispersed all over the world.

After the judgment, the sign of judgment (tongues and the other gifts) was no longer needed, so it must have passed from the church. This seems to agree with the thinking of the writer to the Hebrews, who wrote in A.D. 68 or 69, and seemed to be unaware of the existence of the miraculous gifts in the church at that time (cf. Heb. 2:3, 4).

8

Factors relating to the foundation period of the church

I believe that the New Testament teaches that the gift of tongues was related to the foundation period of the church. We are now in the period of the superstructure since the foundation laid by Christ and the apostles already has been established. It therefore would seem necessary that the gifts uniquely related to the foundation period would cease. One writer has said that "tongues were the swaddling clothes of the infant churches." Now that the church has come to maturity, the gift of tongues is no longer necessary. There are three basic considerations that seem to connect the gift of tongues specifically with the foundation period of the church (i.e., the first century) that have a direct bearing on the question of the cessation of the gift of tongues.

INFANCY AND MATURITY

The first important factor is that the New Testament writers viewed the gift of tongues as a gift connected with the infancy period and thought that it would pass away when the church became "mature."

> But where there are prophecies, they will cease; where there are tongues, they will be stilled; when there is knowledge, it will pass away.... When I was a child, I talked like a child, I reasoned like a child. When I became a man, I put childish ways behind me (1 Cor. 13:8, 11).

Paul uses the figure of a child growing up as an illustration of the church of Christ moving from childhood to maturity. The middle voice of the verb translated "be stilled" indicates that tongues would die out in and of themselves.

When was this to occur? According to verse 11 it would be as the church was coming out of its period of infancy. So when was that?

The language used in the Scriptures should help answer that.

Nepios becomes aner

The Hebrews had nine words for the growth of a child from infancy to manhood:[1]

(1) *jeled* — a newly born child (Exod. 2:3, 6, 8).

(2) *jonek* — a suckling (Ps. 8:2). The Hebrews nursed their children until the age of two and sometimes three.

(3) *olel* — still a suckling, but beginning to ask for solid food (Lam. 4:4).

(4) *gamul* — a weaned child (Ps. 131:2).

(5) *taph* — a child that clings to its mother or still chooses to remain in the same geographic location (Jer. 40:7).

(6) *elem* — becoming firm and strong (Isa. 7:14). It would cover the years from six through fourteen approximately.

(7) *naar* — a youth. This refers to the beginning of maturity when the child begins to become independent of his parents. It has the idea of "to shake off."[2]

(8) *bachur* — the ripened one (Jer. 15:8; 18:21). This is a young man ready for military service.

(9) *ish* — a man.

The first six words refer to the child's period of dependence; the Greek words used for this general period are *nēpios, brephos,* and *paidon.* Paul used

---

1 Alfred Edersheim, *Sketches of Jewish Social Life* (Grand Rapids: Wm. B. Eerdmans, 1967), pp. 103, 104.
2 Brown, Driver, Briggs, *Hebrew and English Lexicon of the Old Testament* (London: Oxford University Press, 1966), p. 654.

nēpios in 1 Corinthians 13:11. It carries the notion of weakness[3] and, note carefully, dependence.[4] The last three Hebrew words are covered by the Greek word, *aner*, "man" ("when I became a *man*," *aner*, 1 Cor. 13:11).

We saw that the transition from *nēpios* to *aner*, from infancy to manhood, involved a "shaking off" of the parental restrictions and the formerly dependent status. To become a man was to become independent, on one's own. This idea probably is what is behind the phrase in Genesis 2:24:

> For this cause a man shall leave his father and his mother, and shall cleave to his wife; and they shall become one flesh.

Jesus repeats this passage in Matthew 19:5. The Greek word he uses for "leave" is a strong word emphasizing a decisive severance. It spoke of a complete break with dependency upon the parents and a setting up of an independent family unit.

Thus, the church moved out of its infancy period, *nēpios,* and into its manhood period, *aner* when it moved out from under the protective cover of Judaism, breaking completely with i and establishing itself as a new and independen faith. This occurred in A.D. 70 when the Roman general Titus destroyed the city of Jerusalem From A.D. 32 until A.D. 70 the church was consid ered to be another Jewish sect. The early be lievers still worshiped and prayed in the syna gogue and considered themselves to be Jews wh had believed on the Jewish Messiah. With th destruction of Jerusalem in A.D. 70, the churc emerged before the world as a separate and di tinct new faith: the Christians continued as religious body even without the temple and th

---

3 *Theological Dictionary of the New Testament.* ed. Gerha Kittel (Grand Rapids: Wm. B. Eerdmans, 1967), vol. 4, p. 91
4 Ibid., p. 918.

Jewish religious system. The break was now clear. The church was no longer in its infancy. From this we may conclude that the gift of tongues probably passed from the church by A.D. 70.

Paul also seems to associate the movement from infancy to maturity with God's judgment on Israel in 1 Corinthians 14:20,

> Brothers, stop thinking like children. In regard to evil be infants, but in your thinking be adults.

He wanted the Corinthians to think about tongues as adults think about tongues. In the next verses he defines adult thinking,

> "Through men of strange tongues and through the lips of foreigners I will speak to this people, but even then they will not listen to me," says the Lord. Tongues, then, are a sign, not for believers but for unbelievers... (1 Cor. 14:21, 22).

As discussed earlier, this passage speaks of tongues as a judicial sign against the unbelieving nation of Israel. Thus, adult thinking about tongues regards them as a sign of God's judgment on Israel for its national rejection of Christ as Messiah.

And this really is important when we step back for a look at Judaism. Every Jew knew by heart Amos 3:2 which says God had chosen *only* Israel, and Exodus 19:5, 6 in which the Jews are designated God's unique people. Even the pagan nations surrounding Israel knew all about their uniqueness in religious matters. So when an insignificant group of Gentiles in Corinth had the nerve to assert, "We are the people of God," the response of the Jews who heard this was, "You've got to be kidding!" Now what was God going to do for His infant church in the face of the overwhelming size and age of His former vehicle, Judaism! Israel had been established for 1500 years as the center of religious worship. God gave the church the sign gift of tongues as a condemnatory sign against Israel, signifying that God was through with her in this era.

Therefore, the childhood of the church ended when the existence of Israel as a nation ended. Then there was no longer any need for a sign to authenticate the insignificant church, nor for a sign against the extinct Jewish nation. This seems to tie the infancy period of the church to the period between its foundation in A.D. 32 at Pentecost to the destruction of Jerusalem by Titus in A.D. 70. It is interesting to note there is not one single reference to the *biblical* gift of tongues (as defined in chapter 1) anywhere after A.D. 70.

Concerning the association of the gift of tongues with the infancy of the church, the great scholar Richard Trench says,

> Miracles, says Fuller, are the swaddling clothes of the infant churches; and, we may add, not the garments of the full grown. They were the proclamation that the king was mounting his throne; who, however, is not proclaimed every day, but only at his accession; when he sits acknowledged on his throne the proclamation ceases.[5]

TONGUES AND PROPHECY

The second major consideration from the foundation nature of the gift of tongues is its intimate association with the gift of prophecy. Prophecy i designated as a gift of the foundation period and passed from the church in the first century. The New Testament seems to teach that tongues woul pass at the time of the passing away of prophecy therefore, the gift of tongues also ceased by th end of the first century.

This argument is based upon an analysis of th Greek verbs in 1 Corinthians 13:8. This can be: be seen by setting up the analysis on the follow ing chart.

---

[5] Richard Chenevix Trench, *Notes on the Miracles and Par bles of Our Lord* (Westwood: Fleming H. Revell, 1953), p. 5

Spiritual gift	English word for its cessation	Greek verb	Tense	Voice	Meaning
prophecy	cease	katargeo	future	passive	sudden removal, abolish
tongues	be stilled	pauo	future	middle	gradual passing away
knowl-edge	pass away	katargeo	future	passive	sudden removal, abolish

From this table, several observations can be seen readily. First, Paul uses the same verb and the same voice when he refers to prophecy and knowledge, but a different verb and a different voice when he refers to tongues. This seems to be significant in view of the fact that tongues lie between prophecy and knowledge in the list. It appears that Paul is indicating that tongues somehow are different. Why? First of all, the change in voice tells us that Paul expected tongues to die out by themselves. The passive voice indicates that the subject receives the action: the middle voice stresses the personal involvement of the subject in the action of the verb. So Paul states that as far as knowledge and prophecy are concerned, God will intervene and simply remove them from the church. Tongues, on the other hand, will not need any direct intervention by God; they will simply die out in and of themselves. The word used for the passing away of knowledge or prophecy could be translated "abolish."[6] Again, this helps to stress the intrinsic nature of the passing away of tongues in contrast to the abrupt removal

6 Walter Bauer, *A Greek-English Lexicon of the New Testament,* translated by William F. Arndt and F. Wilbur Gingrich Grand Rapids: Zondervan, 1957), p. 23.

of prophecy. As we move to the following verse, Paul seems to move beyond the time of the passing away of tongues to the time of the sudden removal of knowledge and prophecy. Knowledge and prophecy are two gifts associated with the impartation of additional divine revelation. Once revelation is complete, these gifts would no longer be needed. Tongues, on the other hand, was a gift which was a sign authenticating the messengers who were giving the new revelations and hence, once the messengers had been authenticated one by one, tongues could gradually pass away. The fact that Paul omits the mention of tongues in 1 Corinthians 13:9 implies that in his thinking they would pass earlier in and of themselves before the passing away of the other gifts mentioned in that verse, i.e., knowledge and prophecy.

I haven't said when prophecy passes away. All I'm stating here is that it appears that tongues will pass first. Are there any passages of Scripture that confirm the conclusion that the gift of prophecy passed from the church in the first century? If there are such passages, then we will have to conclude that tongues also passed.

The passing of prophecy

The major passage to be considered in this connection is Ephesians 2:20 where Paul says that all believers in Christ are

> built on the foundation of the apostles and prophets with Christ Jesus himself as the chief cornerstone. In him the whole building is joined together and rise to become a holy temple in the Lord.

It seems clear that the prophets referred to here are not Old Testament prophets because Paul says apostles, *then,* prophets. The word order is significant. If he was referring to Old Testament prophets, he probably would have said prophets

114

then apostles. Also, the parallel passage in Ephesians 4:8, 11 identifies the prophets as those whom the *ascended* Christ gave to His church. When Paul lists the spiritual gifts in 1 Corinthians 12:28 he follows the same sequence,

> And in the church God has appointed first of all apostles, second prophets. . . .

Note that these are appointed *in the church*. Thus he is speaking of New Testament prophets again using the same parallel structure as in Ephesians 2:20 and 4:11. Furthermore, all three passages are by the same author, in the same order, on the same subject — spiritual gifts.

The church in Ephesians 2:20 is compared to a building which has a foundation and a superstructure. Paul says the foundation represents the first period of church history, Christ and the apostles and prophets. The superstructure represents the succeeding centuries since the first century.

2nd-20th centuries	ALL CHRISTIANS SINCE APOSTLES AND PROPHETS	superstructure
1st century	APOSTLES AND PROPHETS	foundation

We are now in the period of the superstructure and not of the foundation. Once the superstructure of a building is laid down upon the foundation, you don't relay the foundation. Prophecy was the foundation, so we can't go back to that. We are above the foundation now. This text is saying, then, that the gifts of apostleship and of prophecy passed during the foundation period of the church.

This view is validated by the fact that the gift of apostleship passed because of the requirements for its possession. (For example, to be an apostle

115

you had to have seen Jesus alive after the resurrection, 1 Cor. 9:1.) Since apostles are here connected with prophets as being in the foundation stage, and one having passed, apostleship, we assume that the other has as well. This brings us back to the gift of tongues. 1 Corinthians 13:8, 9 seems to indicate that tongues passed before prophecy. Since prophecy passed in the first century, tongues must have passed in the first century as well.

It is possible to view the verb analysis in 1 Corinthians 13:8 in a different way. It could be that Paul is saying that when prophecy and knowledge pass away, then tongues will die out in and of themselves because they will no longer be needed as authenticators of the other two gifts. Either way, the verbs indicate that the gift of tongues will pass *at the time of* the passing of prophecy, which seems to be clearly connected with the first century.

THE INFERIORITY OF TONGUES

Even in the foundation stage of the church, when miracles abounded, tongues was considered an unimportant spiritual gift in comparison with the others. If it was that unimportant in the foundational stage, why is it given so much eminence today? The third factor related to the foundational period that seems to suggest the temporary nature of tongues, is its inferiority in that period. Since it was so unimportant, why should it be continued?

The whole point of 1 Corinthians 14 is to show the inferiority of tongues to the gift of prophecy. Paul brings this out in several ways. In verses 1-12 he notes that tongues are an inferior method of communicating truth to the church. This is true because an interpreter is needed to interpret them

116

but prophecy needs no interpreter (14:2, 3, 6, 9).

In verses 14-19 Paul observes that tongues are an inferior method of worship, prayer, and praise. He says that this is true first of all because the whole personality is not involved (14:14, 15).[7]

> For if I pray in tongue, my spirit prays, but my mind is unfruitful.

Whenever one prays to God, he prays with his human spirit. We come into contact with the things of the Holy Spirit through the agency of our human spirits (1 Cor. 2:11). So, whether a man is praying in a tongue or in his native language, he is praying in his human spirit. To pray in the spirit is not praying in tongues, but simply praying, period!

> So what shall I do? I will pray with my spirit, but I will also pray with my mind; I will sing with my spirit, but I will also sing with my mind (1 Cor. 14:15).

Paul says that he will not pray without using his mind. Hoekema comments,

> I believe Paul here means to say, "I will pray in church with my understanding, in a language which every worshipper can understand. When I do this, I will still be praying with my spirit (the spirit which would be exclusively active if I prayed only in tongues), but I will be praying with my understanding also."[8]

So Paul will pray only in such a way that his whole person is involved, i.e., with both his spirit and his mind. To pray in tongues involves only the human spirit. This tendency probably was brought over from their heathen background of ecstatic speech in connection with Diana worship. They were using the legitimate gift of tongues in

---

7 This passage has been developed well by Bill Hogan in a mimeographed paper. This paper can be procured by writing to 7 Reese Avenue, Newton Square, Pennsylvania 19073. The title is "Speaking in Tongues."

8 Anthony A. Hoekema, *What About Tongue-Speaking?* (Grand Rapids: Eerdmans, 1966), p. 82.

the way they used to use ecstatic speech in their pagan worship before becoming Christians. When they prayed in ecstatic speech to Diana, their mind was not engaged. It was this kind of prayer that Jesus had forbidden in Matthew 6:7. They were now praying in the New Testament gift of foreign languages and their mind wasn't engaged either. To pray in ecstatic speech or even in New Testament tongues without engaging the mind is a heathen practice. Yet, isn't this what the twentieth-century tongues movement seems to be advocating?

Tongues also are an inferior method of prayer and praise because no one can enter into praise with you (1 Cor. 14:16-19).

Not only are tongues an inferior method of communication, verses 1-12, and of praise, verses 13-19, but they also are an inferior method of evangelism, verses 20-25. In these verses Paul points out that the unregulated use of tongues will cause unbelievers to think you are mad (1 Cor. 14:23). But prophecy will result in conviction in the heart of the non-Christian. So Paul is showing that tongues are inferior to the gift of prophecy in the area of evangelism.

I'm not saying that God could not have continued the gift of tongues in the church if it were His purpose to do so. I'm only suggesting that the limited value which Paul ascribes to this gift suggests that there would be little worth in having it continued.

9

Factors relating to the closing of the canon

The canon of Scripture (the Old and New Testaments) was completed when the apostle John wrote the book of Revelation in A.D. 90. The gift of tongues was a necessary gift along with the other gifts given for divine revelation during the time when the church had no New Testament in written form. During this period the revelatory gifts provided the source of authority and doctrinal stability that the infant church needed prior to the completion of the New Testament Scriptures. Once the New Testament had been written, the need for these gifts passed, and, therefore, the gifts probably also passed from the church. There are three factors related to the closing of the canon that suggest that the gift of tongues was only temporary.

The Coming of the "Perfect"

A central passage on the question of the cessation of the gift of tongues is 1 Corinthians 13:8-10.

> Love never fails. But where there are prophecies, they will cease; where there are tongues, they will be stilled; where there is knowledge, it will pass away. For we know in part and we prophesy in part, but when perfection comes, the imperfect disappears.

This passage teaches that there will come a time in the history of the church when the gifts of tongues, prophecy, and knowledge will pass. It is here taught that these gifts will pass when the "perfection" comes. What then, does the "perfection" refer to?

The "perfection" — the Second Coming?

The general view held by most scholars is that the perfection refers to the Second Advent of Christ to earth. This, of course, is the accepted view among our brothers in the charismatic movement also. While this is certainly possible, I personally have had trouble making this view fit into the immediate context of 1 Corinthians 13. There are several weaknesses of this view that should cause us to at least give some serious consideration to some other possibilities.

First of all, to consider the perfection as the "perfect" in the absolute sense is foreign to Paul's general usage in the Bible. Normally, the Greek word, *telion,* carries the notion of "wholeness," "maturity," or "that which is complete." If the perfection refers to the Second Advent you then must inject into *telion* a meaning of absolute perfection which is not Paul's normal usage.[1] Furthermore, this usage is more in accord with Greek philosophy than with the New Testament.[2]

Second, to assign the meaning of Second Coming to *telion* doesn't provide an adequate opposite for the "in part" of the preceding verse. Whatever *telion* refers to, it must be the opposite of that which is in part. The idea of "in part" carries the notion of quantity, the opposite then, i.e., the *telion,* must carry the idea of quantity. The notion of perfect, however, suggests quality rather than wholeness or completeness which would be suitable quantitative ideas to contrast with the "in part."

A third reason for doubting that the perfection refers to the Second Coming is the unnatural in-

---

1 Delling, "Telos," *Theological Dictionary of the New Testament,* ed. Gerhard Kittel (9 vols.; Grand Rapids: Eerdmans, 1972), VIII, 73-77.

2 Ibid., 69-72.

terpretation of verse 13 that results.[3] In 13:13 Paul is contrasting the temporary nature of prophecy, tongues, and knowledge with the permanent nature of faith, hope, and love: "And now these three remain: faith, hope and love. But the greatest of these is love." If the phrase "And now" (Greek = *nuni de*) means "now in this present era," then Paul is contrasting between faith, hope, and love which will abide in this present era versus knowledge, tongues, and prophecy which will not. Thus, knowledge, prophecy, and tongues would presumably have died out sometime earlier than the end of the present era, i.e., before the Second Coming. However, if the perfection in 13:10 refers to the Second Coming, then verse 13 would be in contradiction to verse 10. In verse 10 Paul would be saying that these gifts would die out at the Second Coming, but in verse 13 he would be saying that they would die out sometime before the Second Coming. In order to harmonize these two verses, the proponents of the Second Coming view for the perfection must reject the natural temporal meaning of *nuni de* and substitute a secondary logical inference view. Thus when Paul in 13:13 says, "And now these three remain..." he does not mean, "And now in the present time these three remain," but he means to say, "But since the case stands thus, faith, hope and love remain." In other words, the abiding nature of faith, hope, and love are supposedly a logical inference from what has been discussed in the preceding verses. Hence Paul is not contrasting the temporal nature of gifts versus the three virtues (faith, hope, and love) in the

3 Robert Thomas, "Tongues...Will Cease," *Journal of the Evangelical Theological Society*, Vol. 17, No. 2, Spring, 1974, p. 83, 84.

present time, but is simply saying that the virtues will abide forever (both in the present time *and* in eternity) and the gifts will abide only up to the beginning of eternity, i.e., the Second Coming of Christ. In doing this the temporal force of "and now" is placed into the background as it simply becomes a general expression for the conclusion of an argument. In this way verse 13 and verse 10 are brought into harmony.

However, this harmony is at the expense of a natural interpretation of verse 13. There is simply no way that "And now" can be taken as making a logical inference from what precedes. There is nothing in the preceding paragraph (13:8-13) that would give a basis for the inference that faith, hope, and love will remain for all eternity. In fact faith and hope are not even mentioned in the preceding verses. Furthermore, a secondary meaning of *nuni de* must be embraced. Its normal force is temporal. In Attic Greek it means "now, at this very moment, and only of Time."[4] Thayer says that is the force in 1 Corinthians 13:13.[5] Abbott Smith likewise assigns the temporal meaning to *nuni de* in 13:13.[6]

The expression is used nineteen times in the New Testament in places other than 1 Corinthians 13:13. In fifteen of those cases I definitely see a temporal emphasis. Thus, the preponderance of usage suggests the meaning of "Now at the present time."[7] Bauer comments that the *nuni i*

---

[4] John Henry Thayer, *Thayer's Greek-English Lexicon of the New Testament* (Grand Rapids: Associated Publishers and Authors, orig. ed. 1885), p. 430.

[5] Ibid.

[6] G. Abbott-Smith, *A Manual Greek Lexicon of the New Testament* (Edinburgh: T & T Clark, 1937), p. 306.

[7] The temporal force is clearly seen in Romans 6:22; 7:. 11:30; 15:23, 25; 1 Corinthians 5:11; 15:20; 2 Corinthians 8:1 22; Ephesians 2:13; Colossians 1:22; 3:8; Philemon 9, 1

an emphatic form of *nun,* "now."[8] Perhaps this explains the contrast with the "Now" of 13:12. There a different adverb is used, *arti. Arti* always carries the notion of "Now at the present time." By shifting to *nuni de* in 13:13, Paul could be trying to make the temporal force even more emphatic. It is as if he were saying, "Now I know in part; then I shall know fully, even as I am fully known, *but for the present time,* up until the time in which I am fully known, only three things will abide, faith, hope, and love and not the gifts."

The point of the section is to show the superiority of love in that it never fails even though tongues and prophecy cease and even though the present state fails. It is simply not necessary to make the end of tongues the same as the end of the present time or at the Second Coming. Since Paul is trying to prove the superiority of love, it might prove the point better if tongues did cease prior to the Second Coming. Then Paul's meaning would be (1) when tongues cease love will abide, and (2) even when time itself comes to an end, love will abide (see Charles Ryrie, *The Holy Spirit,* p. 91).

Perhaps the major objection to taking *nuni de* as a logical inference is the forced redefinition of faith and hope which result. On the logical inference view faith, hope, and love must continue for eternity in contrast to gifts which will cease at the second coming of Christ. But, at the second coming of Christ there will no longer be any need for hope because what we hoped for will be reality. Thus, faith, too, will no longer be necessary.

Hebrews 8:6; 9:26. The logical force may be observed only in Romans 3:21 (?); 7:17; 1 Corinthians 12:18; 15:20.

8 Walter Bauer, *A Greek-English Lexicon of the New Testament,* translated by Arndt and Gingrich (Grand Rapids: Zondervan, 1957), p. 547.

> Now faith is being sure of what we hope for and certain of what we do not see (Heb. 11:1).

Since at the Second Coming we will no longer hope, and furthermore we will see Christ and the blessings of the kingdom age, faith will not continue. What's more, hope cannot continue if we understand Paul's concept of hope correctly.

> Not only so, but we ourselves, who have the first-fruits of the Spirit, groan inwardly as we wait eagerly for our adoption as sons, the redemption of our bodies. For in this hope we were saved. *But hope that is seen is no hope at all. Who hopes for what he already has?* But if we hope for what we do not yet have, we wait eagerly for it patiently (Rom. 8:23-25).

Thus, biblical hope involves something that is not seen and something that we do not have. However, at the Second Coming we will see the Lord Jesus and we will have a redeemed body. Now if we accept the logical inference view of *nuni de* then we have the impossible situation of faith and hope continuing for all eternity. However, if we take the normal use of *nuni de*, then Paul is only saying that faith and hope remain *in the present time* in contrast to the gifts which do not remain continuously throughout the present time. Kling, who holds to the logical inference view of "And now" candidly admits, "The chief objection to this construction arises from the fact that Paul elsewhere exhibits to us faith and hope as belonging to the present life in contrast with the future. So in 2 Corinthians 5:7, where 'walking by faith' is opposed to 'walking by sight'; and Romans 8:24, where we are said to be 'saved by hope,' which was hereafter to be merged in sight. Shall we then put the Apostle in contradiction with himself?"[9]

---

[9] Christian Friedrich Kling, *The First Epistle of Paul to the Corinthians,* translated by Daniel W. Poor (*Lange's Commentaries,* 12 Vols.; Grand Rapids: Zondervan, 1960), X, 273.

A fifth objection to equating the perfection with the Second Coming lies in the clear statement of Joel 2:28 that at the Second Coming prophecy will *not* cease but will actually become operative once again. Thus, the perfection must refer to some event prior to the Second Coming or Paul is in contradiction with Joel.

A sixth and final objection to understanding the perfection as the Second Coming lies in the fact that if it does, then the gifts of knowledge and prophecy will remain throughout this present age. These gifts were the vehicles through which divine revelation was imparted. When a prophet or a man with the gift of knowledge spoke with a message from God, it was considered as authoritative as Scripture because the message was a direct revelation. Not every message that a prophet proclaimed was recorded in Scripture, but since their message was the words of God it had the authority of Scripture. If these gifts continue during the present age, then it is possible today for the church to have men speaking with the same authority as Scripture itself. It would mean that revelations and supernatural prophecies are continuing throughout this present age. While these gifts were necessary in the early church prior to the completion of the New Testament canon to provide guidance and doctrinal purity before the written Scriptures met that need, we have no need of these gifts today because we have a completed canon of Scripture. Furthermore, as will be discussed in the following section, there are numerous scriptural indications that indicate that direct revelations from God ceased as a norm of His operation in the first century (cf. Heb. 1:1, 2; Jude 3; Rev. 22:18, 19). Hence, if the perfection refers to the Second Coming, then Paul contradicts himself. In 1 Corinthians 13:10 he is saying that direct revelations from God continue throughout the present age, and in the rest of the Bible he teaches that these things will cease with the completion of the New Testament.

Obviously, this point is based on the assumption that the gifts of knowledge and prophecy were gifts of direct supernatural revelation. If they were not, then there would be no contradiction. Some have maintained that the gift of knowledge is simply the gift of acquiring great learning through study and that the gift of prophecy simply is preaching. Thus, these gifts, defined in this way, could continue throughout the present age and not present any problems related to the closing of the canon. It appears highly questionable, however, that knowledge and prophecy involve only mere learning and preaching. Paul clearly associates the gift of knowledge with revelations and prophecies in 1 Corinthians 13:2 and 14:6. Leon Morris,[10] John Walvoord,[11] Merrill F. Unger,[12] and the article by Bultman in the *Theological Dictionary of the New Testament*[13] all share this view. Bultman comments, "Such knowledge is ecstatic, a mystical vision, and thus it is a seeing in the sense of mystic vision."[14]

The gift of prophecy in the New Testament served to encourage believers (1 Cor. 14:3; Acts 15:32) and to convict unbelievers of sin (1 Cor. 14:24, 25). However, that doesn't tell us what the

10 Leon Morris, *The First Epistle of Paul to the Corinthians* (London: Tyndale Press, 1958), p. 171.

11 John F. Walvoord, *The Holy Spirit* (Findlay: Dunham 1955), p. 178.

12 Merrill F. Unger, *New Testament Teaching on Tongue* (Grand Rapids: Kregel, 1971), p. 83.

13 Rudolph Bultman, "Gnosis," *Theological Dictionary o the New Testament*, ed. Gerhard Kittel (9 Vols.; Grand Rapids: Eerdmans, 1967), I, 710.

14 Ibid.

gift was, it only tells the use to which it was put. The gift itself involved authoritative speaking of the will of God both in foretelling the future (Acts 21:10; Rev. 10:11) and in forthtelling a message from God. This message could be an authoritative exposition of Scripture already written or the impartation of additional revelation (Luke 1:67; Acts 13:1; 15:32; 1 Cor. 14:3). It involved a declaration which could not be known by natural means (Matt. 26:68). This gift, like knowledge, was necessary until the completed canon of Scripture was recorded. It sometimes involved supernatural utterances which were not initiated by the speaker's own will (2 Peter 1:20, 21; John 11:51), but came directly from God through the mouth of the prophet.

We conclude then, that the perfection must refer to some event prior to the Second Coming and cannot equal the Second Coming. If it doesn't refer to some prior event, then in one place Paul indicates that knowledge and prophecy continue throughout the present age (1 Cor. 13:8-13), while the rest of Scripture and the other biblical writers seem to assume the finality of revelation in Christ and His apostles.

It is simply not possible that the perfection can refer to the Second Coming. It's time this seemingly obvious interpretation was set aside. The difficulties presented with this view above should lead us to consider some other possible alternatives. For myself, it appears likely that the perfection refers to the maturity of the body of Christ.

Perfection — maturity of the body of Christ?

If this is the correct notion then Paul is picturing the church growing through progressive

127

stages of development during the present time and gradually coming to full maturity at the Second Coming. Several considerations favor this viewpoint.

First of all, throughout Paul's writings he frequently contrasts perfection (Greek=*telion*) with childhood (Greek=*nēpios*). In each of these instances, *telion* carries the idea of maturity. (See 1 Cor. 2:6 and 3:1.)

> We do, however, speak a message of wisdom among the *mature* (Greek=*telion*) (1 Cor. 2:6).

Just as in 1 Corinthians 13:8-10, Paul contrasts the mature, *telion*, with the infant.

> Brothers, I could not address you as spiritual but as worldly — mere *infants* in Christ (Greek = *nēpios*) (1 Cor. 3:1).

Consider also the contrast in Ephesians 4:13, 14. Here the Greek word *telion* is used once again in contrast with the word *nēpios* just as in 1 Corinthians 13:10, 11.

> Until we all reach unity in the faith and in the knowledge of the Son of God and become *mature (telion)*, attaining the full measure of perfection found in Christ (Eph. 4:13).

Now, note the contrast in Ephesians 4:14,

> Then we will no longer be *infants (nēpios)*, tossed back and forth by the waves, and blown here and there by every wind of teaching and by the cunning and craftiness of men in their deceitful scheming.

Finally, let's consider a passage outside the writings of Paul, in Hebrews 5:13, 14.

> Anyone who lives on milk, being still an infant *(nēpios)*, is not acquainted with the teaching about righteousness. But solid food is for the mature *(telion)*. . . .

Second, in much of the Greek literature outside of the Bible the same contrast is often found. In the writings of Polybius for example, reference is made to Philip of Macedon who had showed him self to be not an infant *(nēpios)*, but a mature man *(telion)*.[15]

A third reason for viewing the perfection as the maturity of the church is found in the many parallels with Ephesians 4:1-16 and 1 Corinthians 12-14. In both passages Paul is talking about infancy *(nēpios)* contrasted with maturity *(telion)*. Also, in both passages he is using the figure of speech of a "body" in describing the mutual interdependence of the various members of the church of Christ. He is in both cases talking of the growth to maturity of the body. Furthermore, the basis for the unity of the believers in the body is the unity of the Trinity in both passages (Eph. 4:4-6; 1 Cor. 12:4-6). The centrality of love is stressed in both passages also (Eph. 4:4, 5, 15, 16; 1 Cor. 13:13). These parallels are too direct to be coincidental. We conclude then, that the perfection in 1 Corinthians 13:10 is the same as it is in Ephesians 4:13, the maturity of the body of Christ. Paul didn't know whether that maturity would reach its absolute state at the second coming of Christ in his lifetime or whether it would be only a relative maturity characterized by the completion of knowledge and prophecy and independence from Judaism in the temporal state. As it turned out, relative maturity was in view, because Christ did not return in Paul's lifetime.

Well, what marks out infancy and maturity? These passages give some clues. One central idea is knowledge. The infant is characterized as slow to learn and lacking knowledge in Hebrews 5:11, 12. The mature man in 1 Corinthians 2:12 understands the deep things of God and the wisdom that has been hidden (1 Cor. 2:7). The same thing characterizes the mature body in Ephe-

---

15 Delling, VIII, 76.

sians 4:13; they have a unity of faith and knowledge. This is the same notion discussed in 1 Corinthians 13:8-10. They have only partial knowledge now, but when the church comes to the perfection, i.e., maturity, they will have complete knowledge.

The central characteristic of infancy, apart from lack of knowledge, seems to be dependency. This is brought out in Ephesians 4:14 where the infant is totally dependent upon the body for his stability. He is tossed to and fro by waves of doctrine, etc., unless he has a mature body to lean on. Thus, if we were going to look for some key ideas to indicate to us when the church moved out of its infancy period and into its maturity period, we should look for a time in the life of the church when it moved out of dependency and lack of knowledge and into independence and complete knowledge. In fact, Paul clearly identifies the perfection as the opposite of that which is in part. That which is in part (1 Cor. 13:9) is incomplete knowledge and prophecy. The perfection, then, would be the opposite of that, or complete knowledge and prophecy. I am anticipating myself here, but this text would seem to imply that the maturity of the church arrived when knowledge and prophecy were completed. This would of course be the closing of the canon in A.D. 90 when John wrote the book of Revelation. At that time the two ingredients for maturity had been reached. The church was no longer dependent upon Judaism but had emerged from the world as an independent entity and was no longer counted as a Jewish sect. This occurred in A.D. 70 when Titus destroyed Jerusalem. Also, the church now had the full knowledge characteristic of maturity in that a completed canon of Scripture was theirs. The move from dependence to independence was the subject of the preceding chapter. Here, we are focusing on the movement from partial knowledge to full knowledge.[16]

Thus, when Paul anticipated the arrival of the perfection, he specifically had the idea of maturity in mind. However, maturity carries with it the ideas of a break with the state of dependency and having knowledge. He did not have the closing of the canon specifically in mind when he wrote I Corinthians 13:8-10. He did maintain the possibility, however, that the ultimate maturity of the body of Christ would be reached in his lifetime. It is to this ultimate maturity that he refers in 13:12 when he says,

> Now we see but a poor reflection; then we shall see face to face. Now I know in part; then I shall know fully, even as I am fully known.

"If events had turned out thus, the first century church would have gone immediately from its condition of dependence on divine revelation still being unfolded through prophecy and knowledge, into its condition of ultimate understanding in the presence of Christ."[17]

Paul also realized that the second coming of Christ may not occur in his lifetime. Then the maturity that the church entered in the present time would be relative and not absolute. This seems to be what is behind the illustration in 13:11.

> When I was a child, I talked like a child (tongues), I thought like a child, I reasoned like a child. When I became a man, I put childish ways behind me.

In other words, if the Lord delayed, the church

---

16 For a full discussion of the biblical and extra-biblical evidence for equating the *telion* with the maturity of the church, see the article by Robert Thomas mentioned above (footnote 3). I have borrowed heavily from this article in this discussion.
17 Thomas, p. 88.

would move into manhood in a relative sense and would put away the things of childhood, i.e., dependence and incomplete revelatory gifts (knowledge, tongues, and prophecy). Paul was perfectly aware that new revelation was being given and that new Scripture was being written. He counts Luke's writings as Scripture (1 Tim. 5:8); he considered himself to be involved in imparting new Scripture (1 Cor. 2:13-15); Peter seems to have counted Paul's writings as equal with the Old Testament Scriptures and thus Paul was certainly aware of this judgment by the Twelve (2 Peter 3:15, 16). Paul knew that as this process of adding new Scripture continued, this growing canon would some day reach completion, like its Old Testament counterpart, and a new stage in the church's maturity would result. This is comparable to the adult he describes in 13:11.

Summing up Paul's thought in 1 Corinthians 13:8-13 we may detect three phases in the growing maturity of the church. Phase I involved the infancy period of shelter under the umbrella of institutional Judaism and when direct revelations were being given prior to the completion of the canon (13:9-11). Phase II would be the entire interadvent period during which faith, hope, and love remain but not the temporary gifts (13:13). Phase III covers the period following the Second Coming when not only have the temporary gifts ceased but faith and hope as well, and the church has moved into full maturity (13:12). "By comparing phenomena pertaining to these three periods, Paul declares the temporal superiority of love: The greatest of these is love, because love never comes to an end. Tongues...will cease, says Paul, 'with whatever comes first: the passing from childhood to adulthood at the completion of the canon and the break with Judaism or at the return of Christ. No matter which comes first, the greatest is still love.' "[18]

THE FINALITY OF JESUS CHRIST

For fifteen hundred years God was involved in the process of communicating especially to men through words in the Bible. We sometimes call this "special" revelation in contrast to God's "general" revelation of Himself in nature. The endpoint of this process culminated in the Lord Jesus Christ. When Christ ascended to heaven special revelation did not cease immediately. The New Testament was written. But that revelation, the New Testament, was simply descriptive and interpretive of the culmination of all revelation in Christ. Thus, the apostles were part of God's final word to man in the person of Jesus. Before Christ came everything was preparation. The whole Old Testament pointed toward and anticipated His arrival. After Christ departed, everything pointed back toward Him. History has been called His story because He is the fulcrum around which our calendar revolves. The Scriptures of the New Testament complete God's last word to us in His Son. Those Scriptures were then being produced, and they are now being applied. New elements of special revelation can no longer be added, for Christ has come, His work has been done, and His Word is complete. The Bible clearly teaches that the complete revelation of God is given in Christ. Because Christ is all in all, and all revelation and redemption alike are summed up in Him, it would be inconceivable that either the revelation or its accompanying signs should continue after the completion of that great revelation with its accrediting works by which Christ has

18 Ibid., p. 89.

been established in His rightful place as the culmination and climax and all-inclusive summary of the saving revelation of God, the sole and sufficient redeemer of His people. This line of reasoning can perhaps best be expressed in the following syllogism:

Major premise: All direct revelations from God ceased with the completion of the canon.

Minor premise: Tongues is a direct revelation from God.

Conclusion: Tongues ceased with the closing of the canon.

If the major premise and the minor premise are valid, the conclusion must of necessity follow. Since the minor premise is generally agreed upon, let's examine the major premise. Is God supernaturally imparting revelation beyond what He communicated through Christ and the apostles? Several Scriptures seem to indicate that this is no longer God's pattern.

The keynote of the book of Hebrews is the finality of the Son of God. Consider the opening verses.

> In the past God spoke to our forefathers through prophets at many times and in various ways, but in these last days he has spoken to us by his son... (Heb. 1:1, 2).

Speaking in prophecies and in various ways (visions, dreams, knowledge, etc.) were part of how God operated in the past. But now He *has spoken* to us in a Son. The Greek verb translated *has spoken* is an aorist which in this context emphasizes a completed and final action that is nonrepeated. God *has spoken*. He has said what He intended to say. As pointed out above, God's last word in His Son included the testimony of the apostles to the Son. God is not speaking in tongues, prophecies, special revelations, etc., today because he *has spoken* in His Son. Thus revelation has ceased, therefore tongues as a means and authenticator of special revelation also ceased.

In Jude 3, Jude declares that *the* faith, i.e., the body of doctrine and teaching *in the process of being communicated* by Christ and the apostles (Revelation had not yet been written when Jude wrote in A.D. 70) has been entrusted to the church "once and for all."

> . . . I felt I had to write and urge you to contend for the faith that God has once for all entrusted to the saints.

Jude viewed the message coming through Christ and the apostles as *a once and for all* message. He viewed it as final, complete, and not to be added to.

It was this kind of thinking that led John to write concerning the book of Revelation,

> I warn everyone who hears the words of the prophecy of this book: If anyone adds anything to them, God will add to him the plagues described in this book (Rev. 22:18).

While this applies specifically only to the book of Revelation, it reflects the consciousness of the early church that the revelations coming through Christ and the apostles were not to be added to.

Jesus Himself announced this to His disciples when He pre-authenticated the New Testament writings by announcing that all things (John 14:26), and all truth (John 16:12, 13) would be communicated through Christ and the apostles. In other words, special revelation would be completed during their lifetime in the writing of the New Testament. Since tongues was a means of the communication of all truth, when all truth had been communicated when God had completed

His revelation in Christ, the gifts of tongues, knowledge, and prophecy passed from the church.

Tongues Mentioned Only in the Earliest Books

A third consideration arguing for the cessation of the gift of tongues is the lack of mention it receives in the latter books. 1 Corinthians was not penned later than A.D. 57, at the end of Paul's three-year ministry in Ephesus (Acts 20:31; 1 Cor. 16:5-8). It is one of the earliest of the Pauline letters. When it was written there was no New Testament in existence, except James and 1 and 2 Thessalonians. Even these books had extremely limited circulation.

> So for practical purposes of instruction and edification the early church had only the Old Testament Scriptures plus what New Testament truth could be communicated directly by the Spirit through special and temporary gifts like knowledge, tongues, interpretation of tongues, prophecy, and specially gifted men like apostles and prophets (1 Cor. 12:28; Eph. 4:11).[19]

Because of this, tongues are mentioned only in the earliest lists of spiritual gifts (1 Cor. 12:8-11). When you look at the later lists (Rom. 12:4-8; Eph. 4:8-12), these gifts aren't even mentioned. The gifts of prophecy, tongues, and knowledge in the list of 1 Corinthians 12:8-11 and 12:28 were divinely designed for a special function in the early church before the New Testament revelation was available for the instruction and edification of God's people. This fact, plus the silence of the later books, indicates that the gift of tongues was passing away.

[19] Unger, p. 82.

10

Factors relating to the authentication of Christ and His apostles

One of the major purposes of the gift of tongues and the other miraculous gifts in the first century was to verify that Christ was God and that His apostles were the messengers of the new era. Furthermore, the New Testament teaches that these gifts were imparted only through the agency of an apostle. Thus, when the apostles died, the gift which was imparted only by them also died. There are three factors related to this authenticating purpose that suggest that the gift of tongues passed from the church in the first century.

THE GIFT OF TONGUES IS NO LONGER NEEDED

According to the Bible, the need for miracles is fourfold. Whenever God began to move in a miraculous way in biblical history, we are able to discern four common purposes. First, miracles (like tongues) were used to introduce a new era of revelation. Thus, the miracles of Moses' time introduced the Ten Commandments, the new nation of Israel, the Tabernacle, the sacrifices, the priesthood, and all of the new revelations of the Jewish dispensation. The miracles of Elijah and Elisha were a revival of the prophetic era. The Jewish dispensation consisted of the law and the prophets. Miracles introduced both of these institutions. Finally, of course, miracles introduced the new era of the church when the One of whom the law and the prophets spoke had come.

Second, miracles were used to authenticate the messengers of the new era. Thus, Moses and Joshua (Exod. 4:1-8), then Elijah and Elisha (1 Kings 17:24), and finally Christ and the apostles (John 10:25), were all attested by the miracles God performed through them.

Third, miracles were used to authenticate the message of the new messengers. God has given only three periods of extensive new revelation. Twenty percent of the Old Testament is concerned with one of these periods, Moses and Joshua. The message itself must be validated each time that new information from God is given. Miracles were a tool for accomplishing this (Exod. 8:21-27; Acts 14:3).

Finally, miracles were used always for instruction to observers in the new era. The miraculous plagues against Egypt performed by Moses were intended to instruct Pharaoh and the Egyptians as to the futility of their gods. Each plague was directed against a specific god the Egyptians worshiped. Hence, the miracles showed the superiority of the God of the Bible over the gods of Egypt.[1] The diagram following summarizes the biblical teaching concerning the four purposes of miracles.[2]

A careful study of the Scriptures included on the chart will establish that God has always had definite purposes for miracles and when those purposes were fulfilled the miracles ceased.

God has now given us His revelation. He has verified through the gift of tongues that the new era has come, that Christ and His apostles are its messengers, that their message is from God and

---

[1] For an excellent discussion of this see *Moses and the God of Egypt*, John J. Davis (Grand Rapids: Baker Book House 1971), pp. 59-152.

[2] John Louis Booth, *The Purpose of Miracles*, unpublished Doctor's dissertation, Dallas Theological Seminary, Dallas Texas, 1965.

GOD'S FOURFOLD PURPOSE IN MIRACLES				
Miraculous Era	To introduce the new era	To authenticate the messengers of the new era	To authenticate the message	To instruct observers
Moses and Joshua 1441-1390 B.C.	God was forming a nation (Exod. 19:8; 33:13; Deut. 4:6-8; Exod. 6:6, 7)	Moses (Exod. 4:1-9, 29-31; 14:31) Joshua (Josh. 3:7)	To Pharaoh (Exod. 7:17; 8:19) "Let my people go!" To Israel (Exod. 6:6, 7; 14:31)	Israel (Exod. 10:1-2; 16:2; 14:13, 14) Pharaoh (8:10, 22; 9:14) Egypt (14:4; 11:7; 9:26) Nations (9:16; Josh. 2:9-11)
Elijah and Elisha 870-785 B.C.	God establishes the prophets (1 Kings 17:1)	Elijah (1 Kings 17:1; 18:36; 2 Kings 1:10) Elisha (2 Kings 5:8)	Forsake your idols and return to the Lord (1 Kings 17:24; 18:36)	Prophets of Baal People of Israel (1 Kings 18:39; 2 Kings 5:15)
Christ and apostles A.D. 28-95	The offer of the kingdom (Matt. 15:24; Luke 4:18, 19; Matt. 4:23; 10:7, 8) The establishment of the church (Acts 15:12)	Christ (Mark 2:7; Matt. 11:4, 5; John 14:11; 20:30, 31; Acts 2:22) Apostles (Heb. 2:4; 2 Cor. 12:12)	The offer of the kingdom (Matt. 12:28; John 10:37, 38) The re-offer of the kingdom and establishment of the church (Acts 3:1-8; 4:16; 8:5-7; Rom. 15:18, 19; Acts 14:3)	The leaders and people of Israel (Matt. 8:26; Mark 6:50; John 6:3-6; Acts 5:1-11)

He has given much instruction, and now those gifts have ceased because the need for them has ceased. God has authenticated these men and their writings, the New Testament Scriptures. Now that the canon of Scripture has been authenticated, God is not going to re-authenticate. Instead He asks us to trust in the testimony of those who wrote the Scripture and in the internal witness of the Spirit.

> . . . blessed are those who have not seen and yet have believed (John 20:29).
> We live by faith, not by sight (2 Cor. 5:7).

These two Scriptures give God's order for this age.

Furthermore, Peter tells us that the word of the Scriptures in the completed canon is "more sure" than any miraculous sign manifestation (2 Peter 1:15-21). He points out that it is even more sure than the transfiguration experience in Mark 9:1-13 which he personally witnessed. Yet he says he has greater trust in what is written in Scripture than in this tremendous experience! In other words, once the Scriptures are completed, we no longer need any authenticating gifts because we have a canon of Scripture which is more sure than any miraculous sign. Therefore, the gift of tongues passed by the time of the completion of the canon.

Some have objected to this line of reasoning on the grounds that the need in the twentieth century is just as great as it was in the first century. The Bible still needs authenticating, they say.

> And to say that their continuance was necessary only during the initial era of the Church would raise a further question: if useful then, why not also during the succeeding eras of the church.[3]

Two things might be said in response to this. First, as pointed out above, the pattern of the Bible connects these miracles with a specific kind of need. What new era is being introduced right now? What new messengers are being introduced in the twentieth century? What new revelation

3 Alva J. McClain, *The Greatness of the Kingdom* (Chicago: Moody Press, 1968), p. 410.

from God needs to be authenticated? There is no new era and there will not be until *after* the second coming of Christ. There is no new messenger and no new message. Therefore, for sign manifestations to continue into the twentieth century would violate the usage by God of these manifestations as revealed in the biblical pattern.

Second, as pointed out in John 20:29 and 2 Corinthians 5:7, sign manifestations are not God's norm for this age. It always has been the mystics' dream that God should give a private revelation of Himself to each individual throughout the whole of human history.

> As Abraham Kuyper figuratively expresses it, it has not been God's way to communicate to each and every man a separate store of divine knowledge of his own, to meet his separate needs; but He rather has spread a common board for all, and invites all to come and partake of the richness of the great feast. He has given the world one organically complete revelation, adapted to all, sufficient for all, provided for all, and from this one completed relevation He requires each to draw his whole spiritual sustenance. Therefore, it is that the miraculous working which is but the sign of God's revealing power, cannot be expected to continue, after the revelation of which it is the accompaniment has been completed.[4]

So says B. B. Warfield, the great biblical theologian of the twentieth century.

Thus, all of the credentials and authority of the first preachers of Christianity did not need continual repetition from age to age. One age of miracles, well authenticated, is sufficient to establish the divine origin of the message. This is true in a human court of law. We do not require an indefinite series of witnesses to receive testimony as valid. "By the mouth of two or three witnesses"

---
[4] B. B. Warfield, *Counterfeit Miracles* (New York: Charles Scribner's Sons, 1918), pp. 26, 27.

the facts are established. The case once decided is not reopened.[5]

The Sign Gifts Were Imparted Only
by the Apostles

The miraculous gifts were given sovereignly by God, but only through the agency of the apostles. Therefore, when the last of the apostles died, the gifts which were imparted only through them died also.

As far as the scriptural evidence goes, there is not one instance where these gifts were received apart from the ministry of an apostle. For example, in Acts 8:14-17, it wasn't until the apostles Peter and John came, that the sign gifts were imparted during the Samaritan revival. Luke seems to be making a special point of this. The whole purpose of the chapter is to establish the need for apostolic sanction and identification. The basic meaning of the laying on of hands is identification. When Peter laid hands on the Samaritans he was saying that their movement was now identified with the church in Jerusalem. Notice how specific the text is on emphasizing that the gift of tongues comes only through the laying on of the hands of an apostle.

> Then Peter and John placed their hands on them and they received the Holy Spirit. When Simon saw that the Spirit was given *at the laying on of the apostles' hands,* he offered them money and said Give me also this ability so that everyone on whom I lay my hands may receive the Holy Spirit (Act 8:17-19).

You could not have a more definite statement a to how the gift of tongues is imparted. Accordin to Luke it was "at the laying on of the apostle: hands." While there is no specific mention c

5 William G. T. Shedd, *Dogmatic Theology* (3 Vols., Gran Rapids: Zondervan, 1962), II, p. 369.

tongues here, pentecostals argue that tongues must have been present because Simon *saw* some visible evidence that the Holy Spirit had been given. This certainly seems reasonable.

In Acts 10:44 when the gift of tongues is again manifested, note that Peter, an apostle, is the agent through whom God imparts the gift. The same is true in Acts 19:6 where Paul, an apostle, is the agent of the Holy Spirit in imparting the spiritual gift of tongues to the new believers in Christ at Ephesus. Also, in Romans 1:11, the giving of spiritual gifts is associated with the office of an apostle. "I long to see you so that I may impart to you some spiritual gift to make you strong." From this passage we can conclude that it was commonly understood that the spiritual gifts could not be received apart from the ministry of an apostle. If an apostle was unnecessary, why wait for Paul to impart the gifts? Surely, Paul's offer and desire would be rather pointless if anyone there at Rome could impart these gifts.

It appears that in the impartation of the non-miraculous gifts, the presence of an apostle was not necessary (1 Tim. 4:14), but the elders of the local church conferred them. The fact that the Scriptures observe a distinction between apostolic impartation of miraculous gifts and impartation by the elders of the non-miraculous gifts tends to confirm the thesis that the miraculous gifts were uniquely for authentication of the apostles. Of course, it is assumed that even the ability to confer the non-miraculous gifts was granted to the elders by the apostles and hence even this associates these gifts with apostolic sanction.

The fact that the gift of tongues and other miraculous gifts were conferred only through the laying on of the apostles' hands is specifically related to a basic purpose of tongues discussed earlier, i.e., to authenticate the messengers of the new age.

> The apostles performed many miraculous signs and wonders among the people (Acts 5:12).
> The things that mark an apostle — signs, wonders and miracles — were done among you with great perseverance (2 Cor. 12:12).

In the Corinthians passage Paul is defending his apostolic authority and appeals to the evidence of the fact that he worked signs and wonders among them. Unless signs and wonders were uniquely associated with the apostles, this would not be a convincing defense. If these signs were the possession of every believer *apart from apostolic impartation,* Paul's whole argument is meaningless. Thus, we conclude that these sign gifts were uniquely related to apostolic authentication and hence could be imparted only through an apostle. Because these gifts could be given only by an apostle, and since the gift of apostleship passed from the church, we have to conclude that the gift of tongues likewise passed from the church by the end of the apostolic era, the first century.

THE "PAST TENSE" CONFIRMATION BY THE FIRST GENERATION

> ... how shall we escape if we ignore such a great salvation? This salvation, which was first announced by the Lord, was confirmed to us by those who heard him. God also testified to it by signs, wonders and various miracles, and gifts of the Holy Spirit distributed according to his will (Heb. 2:3, 4).

The writer to the Hebrews is writing to a group of second-generation Christians, and he is exhorting them to move on in their faith. Their lack of spiritual vitality concerns him. So in chapter he presents the glories of Christ which were attested by angels. In view of this fact, he says w ought to be especially heedful of the salvation he is offering.

Furthermore, we should not neglect this "so great salvation" because its reality has been *confirmed* by eyewitnesses (Heb. 2:3, 4). He is basing his major argument for their going on with the salvation given to them on the fact that it is a salvation definitely confirmed by first-generation eyewitnesses. It was first spoken by the Lord, and then confirmed to us by the ones who heard him. God also testified to the validity of their testimony (i.e., that of these first-generation eyewitnesses) by enabling them to perform miracles and by imparting to them certain sign-gifts of the Holy Spirit.

The Greek verb in verse 3, "was confirmed," is the Greek aorist *ebebaiothe*. The aorist tense in this context implies a completed, once and for all event in past time. It is emphasizing the unrepeatedness of the event in question. Thus, the confirmation was given and then not repeated. Not only is the confirmation a past-tense event but so is the corroborative witness which God provided in the form of miracles and gifts of the Holy Spirit. This is evident because the Greek present tense participle "testified" *(synepimartyrountos)* describes action contemporaneous with that of the main verb "was confirmed" *(ebebaiothe)*. Thus, when the author of Hebrews wrote in about A.D. 68, both the eyewitness testimony and the miraculous corroboration were past events. The verb tense does not indicate that these things were still in the process of occurring.[6]

Notice that this man is writing to a second-generation group of Christians, and he's trying to get them to move on in their faith. The basis of

---

6 Donald W. Burdick, *Tongues: To Speak Or Not To Speak* (Chicago: Moody Press, 1969), p. 38.

his appeal is the confirmed testimony (through the miraculous gift of the Holy Spirit: tongues, etc.) of the first-generation Christians. Since he is basing his whole appeal on the confirmation of the testimony of first-generation Christians through the sign-gifts of the Holy Spirit, it seems incredible that he would not allude to a second-generation manifestation of the gifts if he knew about them. Could he have cited second-generation manifestations of these sign-gifts, it would have made his argument much stronger. As it is, he has to appeal to first-generation manifestations. It appears that this apostle was not aware of the continued presence of these unusual sign-gifts in A.D. 70 when he wrote the epistle of the Hebrews. Possibly tongues were already beginning to die out "in and of themselves" (1 Cor. 13:8).

11

Factors relating to the historical cessation of the gift of tongues

A casual reading of the book of Acts reveals that something was drastically different between God's dealings with men in miraculous ways in the early chapters compared to the notable infrequency of those miracles in the later chapters. When we enter into the second century, it's a completely new era. Miracles have apparently ceased altogether. It becomes immediately obvious that God has changed His way of working, as the transition was made from the first century to the succeeding centuries. There are two factors related to this observable historical process that suggest that the gift of tongues passed from the church by the end of the first century.

THE CESSATION OF THE OTHER GIFTS AND SIGNS

The New Testament seems to teach that some of the other gifts and signs of the early church passed from the church by the end of the first century. This establishes a pattern for the cessation of the other gifts, such as tongues.

The cessation of prophecy

The biblical evidence for the passing away of this gift was presented in chapter 8 (cf. p. 112). As pointed out in that chapter, the associating of this gift with the gift of tongues would lead one to assume that the gift of tongues likewise ceased.

The cessation of healing

I personally believe that there are times in which God supernaturally heals people today. I know of believers in Christ who have had their backs supernaturally "straightened," who have been healed of cancer and other terminal illnesses in response to prayer. It appears obvious to me that James believed that the possibility of supernatural healing exists for all believers in all generations in response to the prayer of faith offered up by the elders of a local church (James 5:14, 15). But the prayer of a group of elders is an entirely different thing from the New Testament gift of healing which was possessed by certain individuals. An illustration of the New Testament gift of healing is offered in Acts 5:16:

> Crowds gathered also from the towns around Jerusalem, bringing their sick and those tormented by evil spirits, and *all* of them were healed.

In the New Testament, the gift of healing was the supernatural ability to heal *everyone*, regardless of the faith of the one being healed. The apostles, for example, raised the dead. A dead man hardly exercises any faith! If a man were here today with the *gift* of healing, he could walk through a hospital and heal everyone in it. Thus, while God may on occasion intervene and heal today, it seems that the gift of healing has passed from the church. This seems evident from the New Testament indications that this gift was beginning to die out during the lifetime of the apostles.

> A.D. 35 — everyone healed (Acts 5:14-16).
>
> A.D. 60 — Paul was not able to heal Epaphroditus (Phil. 2:25-28).
>
> A.D. 67 — Paul could not heal Trophimus, but left him sick at Melitus (2 Tim. 4:20).

Now Paul, Trophimus, and Epaphroditus were all Spirit-filled men of faith, and yet Paul was unable to heal them. This suggests that the gift of healing was passing from the church during

Paul's lifetime. It is true that Paul healed people around A.D. 60 (Acts 28:9) but he no longer healed *everyone*.

The plain fact of our experience today is that God simply does not heal with the frequency He seemed to in the first century. But even in the first century, Jesus never healed everyone in Palestine. In fact, He healed only an insignificant amount of the pain and suffering He witnessed. Only Lazarus came forth and not the hundreds of other bodies in the graveyard. The brilliant Reformed theologian from Amsterdam, G. C. Berkouwer observes,

> What is asked for in the so-called "faith-healings" is even more than what Christ Himself did, and a universality is claimed for them for which there is no demonstrable grounds in the New Testament.[1]

Thus, only in a limited time period did the ability to heal everyone brought to them seem to be operative among the apostles. By the end of their own lifetimes they were unable to do what modern faith healers claim to be able to do!

Sir Robert Anderson has written a book that ably refuted the critics of his generation. They argued against the miracles of the Bible on the grounds that they never happened in the 1900 years following Christ. He wrote a book called *The Silence of God* in which he shows why God has been "silent" relative to the miraculous outburst of special revelation in the first century. In this book he makes a comment that fitly sums up our discussion of faith healing.

> I know that if in the days of His humiliation this poor crippled child had been brought into His presence He would have healed it. And I am assured that His power is greater now than when He sojourned upon the earth, and that He is still as near

---

[1] G. C. Berkouwer, *The Providence of God* (Grand Rapids: Eerdmans, 1952), p. 228.

to us as He then was. But when I bring this to a practical test, it fails. Whatever the reason, it does not *seem* to be true. This poor afflicted child must remain a cripple. I dare not say He *cannot* heal my child, but it is clear that He *will* not. And why will He not? How is this mystery to be explained? The plain fact is that with all who believe the Bible the great difficulty respecting miracles is not the occurrence but their absence.[2]

Thus, the clear testimony of the history of the church is that the New Testament gift of healing has passed from the church. Since it has passed, we conclude that tongues likewise may have passed.

The cessation of apostleship

The data of the New Testament requires us to assume that the gift of apostleship also passed from the church. This was another supernatural gift like the gift of tongues. The word *apostle* has both a general and a specialized meaning in the New Testament.[3] In a general sense, it was simply anyone who was sent to preach the Gospel. But it also is a specific gift which was given to the Twelve and to Paul. It was the gift of absolute spiritual authority. One of the prerequisites for being the recipient of this gift was that the person had to have seen the resurrected Christ.

Am I not an apostle? Have I not seen Jesus our Lord? (1 Cor. 9:1).

The question requires the affirmative answer and is offered as proof of his claim to the gift of apostleship.[4] In order to have the gift of apostleship, you had to have seen the Lord. This obviously limits the gift of apostleship to the first century. Since prophecy is associated with apostleship in

2 Sir Robert Anderson, *The Silence of God* (London: Hodder and Stoughton, 1905), pp. 27, 28.

3 John F. Walvoord, *The Holy Spirit* (Findlay: Dunham Press, 1958), pp. 175-177.

4 Archibald Robertson and Alfred Plummer, *A Critical and Exegetical Commentary on the First Epistle of St. Paul to the Corinthians* (ICC; Edinburgh: T & T Clark, n.d.), p. 177.

Ephesians 2:20, we conclude that prophecy also passed away. Tongues, prophecy and apostleship all are associated with each other in Ephesians 2:20 and 1 Corinthians 13:8-10. If one passed, they all passed. These passages seem all to correlate and mutually establish the overall conclusion.

The cessation of sudden judgments

A careful reading of the New Testament reveals that in the early days of the church God dealt with sin among believers and among critics of the Gospel in immediate physical judgments. As we approach the end of the first century, however, we find that God ceased to deal with men in this way. Thus, the sign of sudden punishment was passing and this sets a pattern indicating that God's dealing in miraculous ways was changing by the end of the apostolic era. Consider the following passages.

> A.D. 32 — Ananias and Sapphira receive an immediate death penalty from the Holy Spirit for lying (Acts 5:1-11).
>
> A.D. 44 — Judgment on Herod (Acts 12:20-25).
>
> A.D. 56 — Paul speaks of delivering a believer over to physical death because of an incestuous relationship with his stepmother (1 Cor. 5:1-5).

Yet, as we move into the next decade (A.D. 60-70) we find that God is no longer dealing with men in this manner.

> A.D. 64 — Alexander, a blasphemer, was turned over to Satan by Paul and yet three years later we find that he still has not been judged (1 Tim. 1:19, 20).
>
> A.D. 67 — Alexander has yet to be "repaid" for what he did to Paul (2 Tim. 4:14, 15).

Thus, we see that by the end of Paul's life God already was withdrawing the immediate judgment that was so characteristic of the early days of the church.

Arthur Custance has observed that these sudden judgments were intended by God to call Israel's attention to the fact that God was starting a new thing.[5] When God inaugurated the Old Covenant, the law, there were many examples of immediate judgment when it was violated. As the law dispensation progressed, however, the sign of immediate judgment ceased. When the Jews observed the immediate judgments of God visited upon the disobedient members of the early church, they would be reminded of the judgments God called down upon them at the beginning of the law dispensation (Num. 16:28-37). So these judgments not only served the purpose of keeping the church pure at its inception but also served to give notice to Israel that God was once again starting something new, the church age. This would help explain why the sudden judgments ceased. They certainly do not continue today. When Peter's reoffer of the kingdom had been rejected (Acts 3:17-26) and Stephen was stoned (Acts 7), it became clear that Israel had finally and irrevocably rejected her Messiah and was to be set aside temporarily in God's program. Hence, all of the signs, miraculous powers, etc., which had as their primary intent a sign to Israel, began to decrease gradually until finally by the end of the book of Acts and in the epistles we no longer find any emphasis on these things.

The cessation of miraculous prison escapes

In the early chapters of Acts no one witnessing for Christ dies. When God's servants are imprisoned, they are supernaturally released (Acts 5:19, 20). Later, Peter was imprisoned by Herod and miraculously delivered once again (Acts 12:6-10). Paul, too, experienced a wonderful deliverance

5 Arthur C. Custance, *The Silences of God* (P.O. Box 291, Brockville, Ontario, Canada: Doorway Papers, 1971), pp. 30 ,31.

(Acts 16:25ff.).[6] Yet, as the first century wore on, we find that God's servants were protected no longer and were delivered from prison no longer. All of the apostles, except John, died a martyr's death. Both Peter and Paul were imprisoned and beheaded at Rome by Nero.

Thus, we see that there was a discernible difference in the way God operated at the beginning of the first century from the way He worked at the end. God's miraculous ways of working were clearly becoming less and less frequent as the norm of Christian experience. This evidence suggests that the miraculous gifts were passing from the church by the end of the apostolic era and constitutes further evidence that the gift of tongues is no longer in the church today.

Tongues Ceased Historically

In the considered judgment of the leading church historians, there has been no reoccurrence of the tongues phenomenon of the first century in the succeeding centuries. According to 1 Corinthians 13:8, when tongues cease they will *cease*. If it is true that historically the gift of tongues ceased, then we would have to conclude that they are no longer in the church today. To cease in 1 Corinthians 13:8 does not mean to stop and then start again; it means to stop, period!

Often in charismatic writings the claim is made that there have been numerous outbursts of New Testament tongues speaking throughout church history. In a popular book, *They Speak With Other Tongues,* by John Sherrill, a list of such historical outbursts is given.[7] His data is typical

---

[6] Alva J. McClain, *The Greatness of the Kingdom* (Chicago: Moody Press, 1968), p. 409. Also see Custance, pp. 29, 30.

[7] John L. Sherrill, *They Speak With Other Tongues* (New York: Pyramid Books, 1965), pp. 76-78.

of that cited in other books. Several things could be said about these purported outbursts.

First, in general, there is no indication that these irruptions of tongues speaking were the New Testament gift of speaking in foreign languages for the purposes of a judicial sign against Israel. By and large they are simply illustrations of a psychological phenomenon called glossolalia which I will analyze in the following chapter. Also, in none of the cited cases that Sherrill lists did the tongues manifestations contribute anything significant toward a major movement in church history. In fact, the major revivals of church history have either totally neglected tongues or mentioned them insignificantly. Furthermore, the citation of these instances begs the real question. Are they illustrations of the legitimate New Testament gift? If they are simply illustrations of what is going on today and is claimed to be the New Testament gift, Sherrill is arguing in a circle. His citations are valid only if what we witness today parallels the New Testament experience. It is my personal opinion that what we are seeing today is not related in any way to the New Testament gift of tongues! Also, I do not believe that the irruptions of tongues in church history have anything to do with the New Testament gift. It certainly is true that the reported outbursts of miracles occurring in the centuries after the apostolic era are fantastic. They increase rather than decrease. But the issue is, are these reports valid

This point has been thoroughly developed in Warfield's monument to sound scholarship, *Counterfeit Miracles*. He observes that it is unfair to argue against the charismatic movement on the grounds that there are no reported outbursts of tongues after the first few centuries. In fact, his torically, the number of outbursts reported increased to a tremendous degree. Instead of concluding that the reports of miracle working in the church decreased he observes to the contrary,

> whereas the direct evidence for miracle-working in the church is actually of precisely the contrary tenor. There is little or no evidence at all for miracle-working during the first fifty years of the post-apostolic church; it is slight and unimportant for the next fifty years; it grows more abundant during the next century (the third); and it becomes abundant and precise only in the fourth century, to increase still further in the fifth and beyond. Thus, if the evidence is worth anything at all, instead of a regularly progressing decrease, there was a steadily growing increase of miracle-working from the beginning on.[8]

However, Warfield then goes on to devote the rest of his book to the thesis that this "evidence" really is evidence of counterfeit miracles and has no connection with the divine attestations of the first century. A. J. Maclean has reached the same conclusion:

> Moreover, most of the ecclesiastical miracles are mere prodigies, and can in no sense be called signs. In many cases they are demonstrably the invention of later biographers, and contemporary writers show no knowledge of them.[9]

Thus, the examples that Sherrill cites, while numerous, beg the real question, as to whether they are valid. The leading church historians say they are not!

Warfield concludes that the miracles cited indicate a merger of Christianity with heathenism.[10] Many of the miracles cited were used to prove doctrines that are clearly contrary to Scripture.[11]

---

[8] B. B. Warfield, *Counterfeit Miracles* (New York: Charles Scribner's Sons, 1918), p. 10.

[9] *Hastings Dictionary of the Apostolic Church*, ed. James Hastings (2 vols.; Edinburgh: T & T Clark, 1918), vol. 2, p. 42.

[10] Warfield, p. 61.

[11] Ibid., pp. 50-52.

Hence, it is rather unfair of Sherrill and other Pentecostal writers to cite the evidence of ecclesiastical miracles, which, though abundant, is based clearly on superstition and error.

The citations in Sherrill's list are scanty and cover 2,000 years of history. There are often gaps of 500 years or more between the appearance of tongues outbursts. This can hardly be said to argue in favor of the gift remaining in the church. It may argue that God occasionally enables men to speak in tongues, assuming that the cited instances were indeed legitimate manifestations of the New Testament gift. But it no more proves that the gift of tongues is in the church today than does Jesus' raising of Lazarus prove that God's norm in the first century was to raise the dead.

As alluded to above, it should be noted that some of the outbreaks of tongues speaking mentioned by Sherrill occurred in connection with known heretical movements. For example, Sherrill cites a revival led by Montanus in the second century and says that the institutional church of the time declared the outbreak of tongues heretical because it was afraid of "excess." While this was true, the more basic issue was that Montanus was declared to be a heretic for claiming to be the paraclete, or advocate, through whom the Holy Spirit spoke to the church, just as the Spirit had spoken through Paul and the other apostles.[12] He taught that the millennial reign of Christ soon would be set up in Phrygia, and that he would have a prominent place in that kingdom.[13] His voice was as authoritative as Paul's. This was pure heresy, and if that is what comes with the charismatic gift of tongues, then Sherrill shouldn't hav

12 Earle E. Cairns, *Christianity Through the Centuries* (Grand Rapids: Zondervan, 1967), p. 110.

13 Ibid.

cited it as an example that the New Testament gift of tongues has not died out.

Philip Schaff, the acknowledged dean of church historians, says that historically the gift of tongues passed from the church at least by the time of Chrysostom.[14] He says that analogous phenomena of an inferior kind to the New Testament gift of tongues, and not miraculous, yet serving as illustrations, either by approximation or as counterfeits, appeared from time to time in seasons of special religious excitement.[15] He mentions that this phenomenon has occurred among the Mormons and other non-Christian sects.[16] He is referring to ecstatic utterances or gibberish.

In the fourth century, Chrysostom (A.D. 347-407), one of the early church fathers in the Eastern Church, testifies that that gift of tongues had passed by his time. In his writings on 1 Corinthians 12 he said,

> This whole place is very obscure; but the obscurity is produced by our ignorance of the facts referred to and by their cessation, being such as then used to occur, but now no longer take place.[17]

Augustine, a contemporary of Chrysostom, living from A.D. 353 to 430, and a leader in the Western Church, was just as definite:

> In earliest times, "the Holy Ghost fell upon them that believed: and they spake with tongues," which they had not learned, "as the Spirit gave them utterance." These were signs adapted to the time. For there behooved to be that betokening of the Holy Spirit in all tongues, to show that the Gospel of God was to run through all tongues all over the whole earth. That thing was done for a betokening, and it passed away.[18]

---

14 Philip Schaff, *History of the Christian Church* (8 vols.; Grand Rapids: Eerdmans, 1910), vol. 1, p. 236.

15 Ibid., p. 237.

16 Ibid.

17 Chrysostom, "Homilies on the First Epistle of Paul the Apostle to the Corinthians," XXIX.

18 Augustine, "Homilies on the First Epistle of John," VI, 10.

It must be admitted that Augustine's testimony on this point is somewhat confusing. The above citation is from his *Homilies* written about A.D. 390. In later works he seems to contradict himself and cite numerous miracles of the most incredible nature. He apparently was motivated more by a desire to believe than by historical fact as Warfield clearly demonstrates.[19]

Thus, from the first century on in the history of the church until the advent of modern Pentecostalism, tongues speaking is reported with notable infrequency, and then generally in groups whose character gives reason for suspecting the validity of the report of the phenomenon recorded. The question we are made to ask is this: If glossolalia is as important a gift of the Spirit as present-day Pentecostals say it is, why did God allow it simply to disappear from the church?

Pentecostals assert that the reason for this historic eclipse of the gift of tongues was simply that the people of God lost faith. Now that there are men in the twentieth century who are believing God again, the gift of tongues has returned. What this amounts to saying is that during 1800 years of church history, the entire church (with a few minor exceptions) failed to enjoy the fullness of the Holy Spirit. This means that men like Luther and Calvin, Wesley, Whitefield, John Knox, Augustine and others were not men of as great a faith as the charismatics today. Furthermore, no one of the major movements of the Spirit in church history had tongues associated with it. It seems incredible that God would leave His church so impoverished for so long!

Therefore, as far as the leading Christian historians know, no parallel phenomenon to the

19 Warfield, pp. 38-45.

New Testament gift of tongues has occurred. The outbreaks generally cited as parallel often led to heresy and fanaticism. So, we may conclude that the indictions of Scripture fit the experience of history and combine to affirm that the gift of tongues passed from the church in the first century.[20]

"But It's the Last Days..."

The writings of charismatic leaders often contain two scriptural arguments for the continuance of the gift of tongues.

The latter rain?

In Joel 2:28 the prophet speaks of an outpouring of the Spirit in the latter days. The present tongues manifestations are then "signs of the times" in the view of many charismatic writers. However, as pointed out in a previous chapter (cf. chap. 7, p. 99) the reference in Joel describes a situation that will exist *after* Jesus Christ has returned and Israel is established in her global kingdom. The context of Joel 2 does not allow us to apply this outpouring of the Spirit to events which will transpire *before* Christ returns.

Charismatics often bolster their view by citing Joel 2:23 in which the prophet refers to the "former and the latter rain." The former rain, they say, is supposed to be the initial outpouring of the Spirit (Acts 2), and the latter rain is the present-day manifestations of the Holy Spirit. However, a careful reading of the context will evidence a different conclusion. The former rain

20 A number of extensive studies on the question of the historical cessation of the gift of tongues have been made. Two books might be consulted in this matter: *The Modern Tongues Movement* by Robert Gromacki, Presbyterian and Reformed Publishing Co., 1967, pp. 5-29. Also, *What About Tongue-speaking?* by Anthony A. Hoekema, Eerdmans Publishing Co., 1967, see pp. 9-34.

does not refer to the initial manifestation of the Spirit in Acts 2, but to the riches of the Jewish kingdom under Solomon and David. The latter rain refers to the even greater magnitude of the Jewish kingdom under the Messiah at the second coming of Christ.

It is interesting to note that this is not the first time in church history that charismatic groups have claimed that the charismatic renewal was a sign of the second coming of Christ. Back in the early seventeen hundreds an outbreak of tongues speaking and prophecy occurred among the French prophets in England. They predicted that a certain Doctor Emes, who died December 22, 1707, would rise again on March 25, 1708. He never did. The prophets emphasized the speedy coming of the Lord and the setting up of His personal reign on earth. They explained that the present diffusing of spiritual gifts among them was a sign of the times.[21]

The Holy Spirit or scorpions?

Another passage frequently cited in popular charismatic thinking is Luke 11:12. In this passage, Christ reasons that if a son asks his father for an egg, will that father give him a scorpion? In the same way, charismatics argue, if we ask God for the gift of tongues, and then begin to speak in other tongues, this proves that it came from God and not from Satan, or from psychological causes. But just because we ask God for something, and we get it, doesn't *necessarily* mean that He is the one giving it. Christians sometimes want something so badly that they will ask God for it, and then go out and get what they want. They then thank God that He gave it to them when God may not have wanted them to have

---

21 Warfield, p. 130.

at all. It is my personal belief that the modern tongues movement is largely psychological in nature, and that to a large extent the answered prayer is simply the result of autohypnosis.

An Excursus on Probability

Without a doubt the most controversial and difficult to accept portion of this book is the section in which I have tried to demonstrate biblically that the gift of tongues has passed from the church as of the end of the first century. It is rather strange in view of such arguments as presented above that there is still a resistance to taking them as proof. I do not claim that these arguments prove that the gift of tongues has passed from the church. I do claim that they give a highly probable exegetical basis for believing that it did. When coupling the exegetical arguments with the clear testimony of church history, one wonders why anyone would want to dispute the point. It is this final issue that needs to be discussed here.

All Christians believe unhesitatingly that the canon of the Bible was closed when John wrote the book of Revelation. We all believe that the Bible teaches, and church history affirms, that God is not imparting additional revelation in the final, authoritative form of the New Testament apostles and prophets of old. Yet, how many Christians could prove what they believe from the Bible? Very few. Furthermore, when the evidences are presented from the Bible that the canon is closed, the vast majority of Christians accept these evidences as valid without question. Here is the interesting thing: the evidence that the canon is closed is *much less* impressive, biblically, than is the biblical evidence that the gift of tongues has passed from the church. Yet, people will readily accept the former as true, but resist the latter conclusion. Why? I suggest that the reason is based on experience and concern (legitimately) for unity among the body of believers, and not straightforward interpretation of the Bible. Once a person has experienced something he is convinced is the gift of tongues described in the New Testament, no amount of scriptural argumentation will suffice to convince him that what he has really experienced is merely a psychological phenomenon. Emotions drive a person to accept what the Bible "possibly" says (that tongues is still in the church) rather than opting for what the Bible "probably" says (the gift passed in the first century). Whenever you replace the probable for the possible you are violating a basic principle of Christian epistemology, which if consistently applied, amounts to reducing the truth to an experience of truth, and ultimately leads to all sorts of biblical errors. The fact that something can't be "proven" in the biblical sense is not the relevant question here. If it's probable, then you should act on what is probable, and not let your experience determine what's probable but let Scripture determine what is probable. When you carry this principle of possibility over probability to its logical extreme, you end up with the basic error of the cults. All of the cults base their doctrine on possible interpretations of Scripture. In fact, in the final analysis you can't "prove" that the Bible teaches anything. But this is only a theoretical difficulty, and not a practical one. We all readily admit that if language has any meaning at all, there are certain doctrines which are so highly probable that to reject them would be to violate all known principles of grammar and syntax, not to mention the testimony of the Holy Spirit. For example, we all believe that the Bible clearly teaches that Jesus is God, the second person of the Trinity, and the Savior of the world. However, the Mormons deny this. They take certain passages in the Bible and impose on them "possible" interpretations in order to support their heretical concept of divinity that says that the only difference between Jesus and us is a difference of degree, rather than of kind. Now, why do the Mormons opt for these "possible" interpretations? Is it because the Bible supports them? Hardly! They do it because they have found love and acceptance among the Mormon people, and because Mormonism has had an experiential impact on their lives. What the Mormons do with the deity of Christ is exactly the same *in principle* with what Christians everywhere do when they let experience cause them to opt for a possible, rather than a probable interpretation of Scripture.

Not only are those who have experienced what they think is the gift of tongues motivated this way, but so are those who sympathetically stand on the sidelines. I remember interacting with a university professor who was a gracious Christian gentleman who, after hearing some of the arguments presented above, still concluded, "You just can't prove it." For some reason that seemed to settle the case and justify belief that tongues may be in the church today. When I probed a little further, however, I found that the real reason he tended to cling to the possibility that tongues were still in the church was *experience!* He knew someone who had spoken in tongues, who was a godly person; therefore, his gift was valid, and no amount of scriptural argumentation would suffice to negate it. We have all experienced this. I have. I know many men whom I admire highly who speak in tongues. Furthermore, I'm not aware of anything but good that has come from it in some of their lives. Usually, there is a series of adjectival clauses that describe this godly person who speaks in tongues: he is a consistent witness for Christ, he doesn't discuss tongues with anyone, tongues are not that big an issue for him, he only uses it for personal edification (which, by the way, I tried to demonstrate was the very abuse of tongues the Corinthians were engaged in, cf. chap. 1), he doesn't push tongues on people, and he doesn't live by feelings but by faith. This series of descriptive phrases is used to put all scriptural arguments aside with this kind of logic: "If a man fits the above description, this proves that the gift of tongues he is experiencing is valid or at least establishes that you can't deny the possibility of the genuineness of his gift."

It *may* be true that the gift he is experiencing is valid (for the sake of argument), and it *may* be true that you can't argue against the possible genuineness of the gift. But, if the gift is valid, it is *not* because a godly person has this list of descriptive phrases after his name; it is because the Bible says it is valid. It is my personal conviction that the Bible does not say that. The final test is: What saith the Scripture? A Christian should always opt for what the Bible probably says and use that as a criteria, rather than a list of adjectives or a personal experience. This is not quibbling. This is a central issue in the rift between liberal existential thought and biblical Christianity. We can't be consistent and argue against the liberals, and then turn right around when in our own camp and argue as existentialists rather than exegetes when we are discussing doctrine within the household of faith.

12

What is the tongues phenomenon today?

Something is happening! People from all denominational backgrounds are having their lives revived as a result of receiving the "baptism in the Holy Spirit." If it is true as I have previously argued that the gift of tongues has passed from the church, then how do you account for the widespread outbreak of tongues speaking witnessed in the twentieth century? Didn't Paul say, "Forbid not to speak in tongues"? How then can you forbid what Paul said not to forbid? The answers to these questions will be attempted in this chapter.

First of all, let me say that I personally would not feel free to forbid anyone to speak in tongues. However, if a man under my spiritual authority began to speak in what he thought was the New Testament gift of tongues, I would feel compelled to insist that he exercise his gift in accordance with the New Testament requirements for its use. As long as he was willing to meet those requirements, I personally would have no problem in his speaking in tongues! While in the previous chapters I have argued extensively that the gift of tongues has passed from the church, I do not wish to put God in a box by saying that He could never in His sovereignty cause a man to speak in tongues. This would be one of the second category of miracles described in chapter 6. As God can perform exceptional miracles between the time of Moses and Elijah (like Gideon's fleece) or between Elijah and Christ (like Daniel in the lion's den), so He can do it today. But as I have tried to point out in the previous chapters, it doesn't appear that this kind of miraculous working is God's norm of operation today. The biblical pattern suggests that any occurrence of tongues speaking today would be an exception. Thus, the charismatic movement asserts that what was God's norm of operation in the first century is His norm of operation in the twentieth century. I personally believe that the Bible teaches that what was God's norm of operation in the first century is His exceptional way of working in the twentieth century. God could effect a prison escape in a miraculous way today. In the early chapters of Acts He did it all the time. God can supernaturally heal today, but He rarely does so. It was His norm of operation in the early chapters of Acts. He could possibly cause a man to speak in tongues today, but the Bible teaches that this gift has passed from this church and hence tongues speaking is not to be part of the daily life of believers in this age. However, if a man did speak in tongues today, he would certainly have to exercise his tongues speaking in a manner consistent with the ten scriptural criteria of valid tongues speaking. If he does not meet these tests, then Paul *would* have forbidden him to speak in tongues, and we should too!

The ten tests of valid tongues speaking

If present-day charismatic manifestations of the gift of tongues are valid expressions of the New Testament gift, we should be able to discern the spirits by applying the test of the Scriptures. We can isolate the criteria of Scripture to mark out the true gift, and then compare those biblical criteria with the charismatic movement. If the comparison is found wanting then we must conclude that what is going on today is not the New Testament gift of tongues and should be forbidden. Thus this list of tests provides both an objective test of whether or not a particular manifestation of tongues today is valid and also provides the conditions under which it should be exercised if it is valid.

It must be a foreign language spoken on earth. As pointed out in chapter 1, the New Testament gift of tongues was clearly foreign languages and not ecstatic gibberish. While there may be some instances today where people have spoken in foreign languages, this certainly is not the norm of the charismatic movement. Almost universally, their tongues speaking is simply ecstatic gibberish and nonsense syllables that have no parallel in the New Testament.

Twentieth-century glossolalia has been under study by linguists for many years. The overwhelming conclusion is that when subjected to the test of linguistic analysis, modern instances of tongues speaking fail the test. This conclusion is based upon the following seven items:[1]

(1) The high frequency of repetition in tongues speaking; similar-sounding syllables are repeated over and over.

(2) The similarity of tongues speech to the speaker's own language background.

(3) The excessive use of one or two vowels.

(4) The absence of any language structure. Some may object that not all of the three thousand or more languages in use are known by linguists, and that for this reason, the languages may be real but unrecognized. Such a conclusion is refuted in

---

[1] Donald W. Burdick, *Tongues: To Speak Or Not To Speak* (Chicago: Moody Press, 1969), pp. 59-65.

a letter written to *Christianity Today* by William
E. Welmers, Professor of African Languages at
U.C.L.A. He explains:

> We do know something about representative lan-
> guages of every known language family in the world.
> I am, by no means, unique among descriptive lin-
> guists in having had direct, personal contact with
> well over a hundred languages representing a ma-
> jority of the world's language families, and in having
> studied descriptions of languages of virtually every
> reported type. If a glossolaliac were speaking in any
> of the thousand languages of Africa, there is about a
> 90% chance that I would recognize it in a minute.[2]

(5) The markedly greater length of the interpretation as compared with the tongues utterance.

(6) The inconsistency of the interpretation of
the same phrase or clause.

(7) The predominately King James style employed in interpretations. Does God speak in
sixteenth-century English?

*It must be used as a judicial sign to unbelieving
Jews.* This was the central purpose in the New
Testament. It is difficult to see how that kind of
usage would have any relevance today or under
what circumstances it could occur. I have heard
of instances where a tongues experience was in-
strumental in leading a Jewish person to Christ.
But evangelism wasn't the primary intent of the
gift. The charismatic movement clearly fails this
test in its use of the gift of tongues (1 Cor. 14:
21, 22).

It must be used publicly and not privately.
In the New Testament there is not a single hint
that the gift of tongues was used privately. The
charismatic movement almost exclusively emphasizes its use as mainly for private edification and
devotions. As pointed out in chapter 1 this is

---

2 William E. Welmers, Letter to *Christianity Today*, VII
(November 8, 1963), p. 127.

unscriptural (1 Cor. 12:7; 14:12, 13, 25; Eph. 4:11, 12).

It must be accompanied with a translation. It is not to be used in the church meeting unless it is translated. Even then, it must be a language spoken somewhere on earth, and an expression of thanksgiving to God (1 Cor. 14:28). In fact, Paul requires of the tongues speaker that he have *prior* knowledge of the presence of an interpreter,

> . . . If there is no interpreter, the speaker should keep quiet in the church . . . (1 Cor. 14:28).

Thus, a man was not to speak in tongues and then find out if there was an interpreter present. He must first ask if there is an interpreter present, and if so, he was free to speak in tongues. The charismatic movement has frequently violated this regulation also. I personally have been in many Pentecostal assemblies in which various tongues speakers blurted out in tongues with no prior knowledge of the presence of an interpreter.

It must be limited to three instances of tongues at any one service.

> If anyone speaks in a tongue, two — or at the most three — should speak, one at a time . . . (1 Cor. 14:27).

Most Pentecostal meetings are a gross violation of this sanction. Generally, you'll find many tongues speakers speaking at the same time. I have attended a number of Full Gospel Businessmen's meetings where as many as twenty men were speaking in tongues at the same meeting and in some cases, simultaneously.

It must be done one at a time.

> . . . one at a time . . . (1 Cor. 14:27).

Again, most Pentecostal meetings involve almost everyone speaking in tongues at once.

It must be limited to one interpretation.

> . . . and someone must interpret . . . (1 Cor. 14:27).

The inference in this verse is that there is to be

an interpretation given by only one interpreter. In many Pentecostal meetings today several interpretations often are given of the same tongues utterance.

It must be exercised by men only, in the church. Women are not permitted to exercise the gift of tongues in the church (1 Cor. 14:34). It is significant that a majority of the tongues speakers today are women. In fact, many women pastor Pentecostal churches.

It must be in balanced distribution. There should be a balanced distribution of the gift of tongues among the members of any local assembly. When Paul teaches on spiritual gifts, he uses the illustration of a body. He comments,

> If the whole body were an eye, where would the sense of hearing be? ... If they were all one part, where would the body be? (1 Cor. 12:17, 19).

Since God tempers the body together, and gives it perfect symmetry, why do Pentecostals have a distorted ratio of gifts? According to the New Testament these gifts are distributed by the sovereign choice of God (1 Cor. 12:11). If God were truly the source of these manifestations today, would there not be a balance and a greater presence of the best gifts? God does not create an imbalance, and yet the Pentecostal movement has a body that is ninety percent "tongue." Therefore this movement could not be of God. "Likewise the current emphasis upon the gift of tongues at the expense of the best gifts shows that the Holy Spirit did not create this desire. The Holy Spirit would not emphasize what Paul had deemphasized. Would He give to the modern tongues movement an abundance of the least gift at the expense of the best gifts?"[3]

3 Robert G. Gromacki, *The Modern Tongues Movement* (Philadelphia: Presbyterian and Reformed, 1967), p. 120.

It must be exercised in love. The charismatic movement, in my opinion, has violated the key test — they have not exercised their "gift" in love. There are, of course, many exceptions to this statement, but I still feel it is a valid generalization.

We must remember that 1 Corinthians 13 is not a parenthesis in Paul's argument, but a vital part of it. Too often we read this chapter as a separate love poem, completely divorced from its context. Each of the descriptive phrases describing true love sprung out of an abuse of the gift of tongues that was being evidenced at Corinth. Let's look at a few of these descriptive phrases. "Love is patient" — a tongues speaker will wait his turn to speak and not burst into speaking at any time (1 Cor. 14:27, 28). "Love envieth not" — believers individually should not covet a gift God has not been pleased to give them (1 Cor. 12:7, 11, 18). "Love vaunteth not itself, is not puffed up" — a tongues speaker should never be proud or think he's something special or think he has something that other believers do not. "Love doth not behave itself unseemly" — speaking in tongues should be done decently and in order. Shaking and physical convulsion are unseemly (1 Cor. 14: 23, 40). "Love seeketh not her own" — the modern tongues movement stresses the use of speaking in tongues for personal edification. This is selfish and not the way of love. Self-edification may be a product of the gift, but it should never be the goal (1 Cor. 14:4, 12).

Does the charismatic movement meet the biblical tests?

A casual reading of the above criteria is sufficient to convince anyone that there is something amiss in the twentieth-century manifestations of tongues speaking. As I said above, I would never forbid anyone from speaking in tongues as long as his experience was in line with the New Testament criteria. I am not aware of anyone in the twentieth century who has met these criteria. Are you?

Tongues speaking today simply does not fit the New Testament pattern and hence cannot be considered a continuation of the New Testament gift of tongues. What, then, is the present tongues phenomenon and how can it be explained?

WHAT IS THE TONGUES PHENOMENON TODAY?

Some of it may be satanic

I do not at all think that much of it is satanic. Missionaries often give accounts of pagan cults involved in tongues speaking. This phenomenon occurs completely outside the realm of Christianity altogether. As pointed out previously, the Mormons claim to be able to speak in tongues, as do the Jehovah's Witnesses. The *Encyclopaedia Britannica* cites many instances of tongues speaking in pagan cults.[4] The fact that the experience occurs regularly in non-Christian religions argues powerfully that the tongues phenomenon of the twentieth century is not being produced by the Holy Spirit. People who have no connection at all with Christianity speak in tongues. D. C. Graham tells of a girl in the Szechwan province of China who was possessed by demons and "began to utter words incoherently."[5] Edward Langston says that in East Africa many persons possessed by demons speak fluently in Swahili or English, although under normal circumstances they do not understand either language.[6] Junod reports that among

---

4 *Encyclopaedia Britannica*. 1968 Edition, vol. 22, p. 75.

5 D. C. Graham, *Religion in Szechwan Province, China* Smithsonian Miscellaneous Collections, LXXX, 4, p. 15.

6 Edward Langston, "What Are Demons?" *The London Quarterly and Holborn Review* (January, 1954), p. 30.

the Thonga people of Africa, when a demon is being exorcised the person sings a curative song which he himself composes. Usually the songs are in the Zulu tongue. Even if the person does not know this language it is claimed that he will be able to use it "by a kind of miracle of tongues."[7] As far back as Vergil (70-19 B.C.) there are references to the tongues speaking of the Sibylline priestess on the Isle of Delos. This is described in his *Aeneid*.[8] Today, ecstatic speech is found among the Mohammedans,[9] and the Eskimos of Greenland.[10] Non-Christian alchemists of the middle ages were reported to have spoken in tongues. This caused them to be popularly feared as men skilled in sorcery.[11] The Bwiti cult among the Fang people of the Gabon Republic has been observed speaking in tongues.[12] The parapsychology laboratory of the University of Virginia Medical School reports incidents of occult speaking in tongues. A Turkish actress claims she learns the "language of Jakosta" from a black man she sees in her dreams.[13] Joseph Smith, the founder of the non-Christian sect of Mormonism, taught his followers to speak in tongues in the following manner, "Arise upon your feet, speak or make some sound, continue to make sounds of some kind, and the Lord will make a tongue or language of it."[14]

Therefore, we may conclude that the mere fact

7 Henri Junod, *The Life of a South African Tribe,* p. 45.

8 Vergil, *Aeneid,* translated by James Rhoades, Vol. XII of *Great Books of the Western World,* ed. R. M. Hutchins (Chicago: Encyclopaedia Britannica, Inc., 1952), Book VI.

9 H. J. Stolee, *Speaking in Tongues* (Minneapolis: Augsburg Publishing House, 1963), p. 9.

10 Ibid.

11 Alexander Mackie, *The Gift of Tongues* (New York: George H. Doran Co., 1921), p. 28.

12 William J. Samarin, *Tongues of Men and Angels* (New York: Macmillan Co., 1972), p. 222.

13 Ibid., p. 254.

14 Ibid., p. 53.

that there is an unusual ecstatic utterance, or even a genuine speaking in foreign languages, does not by any means prove that the glossolalia is of God.

Most of it is psychological

It is my personal conviction that the tongues speaking characteristic of the charismatic movement is simply a common psychological phenomenon that psychologists have been studying for years called glossolalia. In fact, psychologists have described this as happening with people with no strong religious convictions at all.[15]

While there is no certain evidence of what causes it, several speculations have been made. Some of it is caused by mere *ecstasy*. The person is in a highly emotional state, and is out of his ordinary frame of mind, and pours forth impassioned utterances.

Another possible cause is *autohypnosis*. Several things combine to produce this. In almost every case there is a sense of frustration and inner conflict. This is particularly acute in Christians, in that their lives often do not stack up with what the Scriptures say is possible. This inner tension sets off a search for the "secret" to the abundant Christian life. Tongues promises to be an end to the tension, and people subconsciously begin to seek it. The autohypnosis is further augmented by the fact that the gift is presented as the acme of Christian experience. To receive it is to gain the hallmark of spiritual prestige, resulting in the feeling of group acceptance and divine approval. Furthermore, everyone around them is assuring them that this gift is the solution to their prob-

---

15 George B. Cutten, *Speaking With Tongues Historically and Psychologically Considered*, p. 157.

lems. This has a powerful effect and will psychologically induce the phenomenon in some people.

A number of Christian psychiatrists have come to the conclusion that the phenomenon is completely psychological. For example, Dr. E. Mansell Pattison, who is a member of the Christian Association for Psychological Studies, and currently an instructor at the University of Washington School of Medicine, said recently:

> The product of our analysis is the demonstration of the very natural mechanisms that produce glossolalia. As a psychological phenomenon, glossolalia is easy to produce and readily understandable.[16]

He adds,

> ...I can add my own observation from clinical experiences with neurological and psychiatric patients. In certain types of brain disorders resulting from strokes, brain tumors, etc., the patient is left with disruptions in his automatic physical speech circuit patterns. If we study these "aphasic" patients we can observe the same decomposition of speech that occurs in glossolalia. Similar decomposition of speech occurs in schizophrenic thought and speech patterns, which are structurally the same as glossolalia. This data can be understood to demonstrate that the same stereotypes of speech will result whenever conscious, willful control of speech is interfered with, whether by injury to the brain, by psychosis, or by *passive renunciation of willful control*. This corroborates our previous assessment that glossolalia is a stereotyped pattern of unconsciously controlled vocal behavior which appears under specific emotional conditions.[17]

So, Dr. Pattison's conclusion is that glossolalia may occur whenever conscious willful control of the brain is interfered with, and that in its present-day form it is usually a psychological accompaniment of intense or ecstatic emotional experiences.

Whatever the circumstances that motivate one

---

[16] E. Mansell Pattison, "Speaking in Tongues and About Tongues," *Christian Standard* (February 15, 1964), p. 2.
[17] Ibid.

person to begin to speak in tongues today, one thing we now know with certainty is that anyone can do it. All that is necessary is that you string together a number of syllables in a random order. For example, while sitting at my typewriter I just produced this illustration of tongues speaking: *shon dai amma bon de kai santi santi alla hambra.* What I just wrote is linguistically no different than hundreds of transcribed illustrations of tongues speaking from all over the world. Thus, I just spoke in tongues! The above conclusion has been carefully documented by a very scholarly book called *Tongues of Men and Angels,* by William J. Samarin. Samarin is a competent linguist who has spent more than thirty years in careful linguistic analysis of hundreds of cases of tongues speaking all over the world. He has attended scores of Pentecostal meetings and has personally interviewed hundreds of persons who have received "the baptism."

While it is true that tongues speaking today is psychological and that it has been under study for years and observed in the lives of nonreligious people, there are no completely satisfactory explanations of what really causes it. It happens to some people who were not seeking it, didn't even know what it was, and who had no inner tensions at all. One day "it" just happens. The latest studies have conclusively demonstrated that there is absolutely no correlation between tongues speaking and "abnormal" behavior.[18] Books written by Christians trying to label Pentecostal brothers and sisters as more "suggestable," or mentally ill, or abnormal, or emotionally immature are based on pure prejudice and lack any verification in sound sociological studies. Since we do not know what

18 Samarin, pp. 18-43.

176

causes the phenomenon, it is pointless to speculate. People from all social classes and levels of society and all religious and denominational backgrounds are involved in the charismatic movement. There are no discernible correlations between social class and involvement. Hence, the derogatory notion that people involved in the movement are of a lower social strata as a group is now known to be completely erroneous. Charismatic people are just plain, everyday, ordinary people who love the Lord and want their lives to count for Him just like other Christians.

Having said that the phenomenon is psychological leaves one question unanswered. How, then, are the genuine examples of foreign languages accounted for? Before commenting on this, let me describe some personal experiences.

A number of years ago I met a man named Dick who spoke in tongues and was quite anxious that I too might receive the "baptism." On a number of occasions as we prayed together he would begin to pray in tongues. This was my first experience in hearing anyone speak in tongues and I must confess it was rather startling to me. As he prayed, there were certain words that I frequently heard: *"shon dai, shanda, ah-shonda."* He claimed it was from the vocabulary of some African tribe. Since that experience I have heard scores of Pentecostal people from all over the United States pray in tongues, and I am continually surprised when I hear exactly the same phrases. Samarin has observed the same phenomenon.[19] I began to doubt that there was any foreign language involved.

On another occasion when interacting with the man I spoke of in the introduction to this book,

19 Ibid., p. 98.

the subject of the foreign language nature of his gift was raised. He said that it was definitely a language. I later wrote him a letter and asked him if he would send me a tape recording of himself speaking in tongues so I could have it analyzed. My thought was to discern whether or not there was any possibility that his gift was the New Testament gift of speaking in foreign languages. He responded by saying he could not comply with my suggestion because to do so would be "tempting the Lord." Apparently, he felt that he was to believe by "faith" that he was speaking in a foreign language and everyone else was to believe it too. While he may have viewed my suggestion as "tempting the Lord," I viewed it as "testing the spirits."

The majority of tongues speakers today, seventy-three percent, believe they are speaking in a language.[20] However, as pointed out above, every study thus far has failed to turn up a genuine example of foreign language. The claims of language rarely are based on analysis by linguists but on the testimony of nonspecialists. One man told me that while he was singing in the shower in tongues, a Polish man overheard him and asked him when he had learned Polish. Of course he never had and this constituted proof that his gift of tongues involved the ability to speak in Polish. I personally have heard many stories similar to this. How is this to be explained?

First, I have had frequent occasion to question the objectivity of the report. The man who was singing in the shower wanted to believe he was speaking in a miraculous language. The Polish man actually overheard a few syllables and some words that resembled Polish. My shower singing

---

20 Ibid., p. 107.

friend desired so much that his "miracle" be reinforced by another person, that he convinced himself that the man's offhand comment implied a whole song in Polish when actually all that was involved were a few similar sounding syllables.

Second, and related to the first point, often these reports of languages turn out to be a few words and not a fluent language.

Third, the few words sometimes spoken or even possible examples of fluent language can be psychologically explained by Cryptomnesia. This refers to the appearance in the conscious mind of what was once stored in the memory and then forgotten. Sometimes, this hidden language is brought to mind under certain kinds of stress.[21] Sometimes it is called exalted memory. While this phenomenon has never been specifically observed within the charismatic movement, it could be the explanation for a number of the unverified reports of languages (i.e., *scientifically* unverified). It could be the explanation for tongues speaking in pagan tribes in which a foreign language reportedly is spoken. Cutten has suggested and cited examples for the ocurrence of exalted memory.[22] In such cases, the speaker retains in his memory utterances in a foreign language which cannot be recalled under normal circumstances. However, when the necessary psychological conditions have been met, the foreign expressions are released, and the person speaks fluently in a language he has never "learned." This phenomenon has been observed many times under hypnosis. A person who has never spoken German suddenly will speak fluent sentences in this language. Always these have been traced back under hypnosis to an

---

21 Ibid., p. 115.
22 Cutten, p. 157.

experience entirely forgotten by the patient's conscious mind, where he either overheard two foreigners talk in that language or even tried to read pages out of a book. This probably is the source of any instance where a foreign language actually has been spoken in a charismatic assembly.

There is a fourth possibility. Some of it may be demonic. Certainly the instances of Africans speaking in English under occultic influence would fall in this category.

In conclusion, it appears that a fair evaluation of all of the biblical and psychological evidence leads one to the conclusion that there is no connection between the tongues speaking manifested in the twentieth-century charismatic movement and the New Testament gift of tongues. The twentieth-century phenomenon is a psychological experience of gibberish and the first-century gift was foreign languages. It appears that the only connection between the two is found in the organ of the tongue itself. After that, all similarities disappear!

13

Corinth repeated?

The aim of this book is to provide an accurate biblical perspective on the tongues speaking movement that is sweeping the twentieth-century Christian scene. Much of the material comes out of the author's own experiences with members of the tongues movement, and from counseling sessions with those who have "received the baptism." There are many sincere and dedicated, as well as fruitful, Christians from all denominations involved in tongues speaking today. In their dedication and fruitfulness, we rejoice. We have no desire to cast any doubt on their sincerity and love for Christ. However, I think it is fitting that in conclusion we call attention to some of the practical considerations that led to the writing of this book. Thus in this concluding chapter we will look at some of the effects that the tongues movement has had on twentieth-century Christianity. As a prelude to this it will be most enlightening to examine first of all the effects this emphasis had on the church in the first century, particularly the church at Corinth.

THE RESULTS IN CORINTH

Emphasis on ecstasy

> Now about spiritual gifts, brothers, I do not want you to be ignorant. You know that when you were pagans, somehow or other you were influenced and led astray to dumb idols (1 Cor. 12:1, 2).

The words "led astray" in the Greek carry the force of being "swept away." Before becoming

Christians, they placed great importance on the spirit sweeping them away in a demonstration of spiritual presence. This was part of the ecstasy of the Greek mystery religions. Apparently, they were still placing importance upon this kind of phenomenon and Paul begins to correct them. This is not a sign of spirituality, he says, but of your heathen days. Although there are many exceptions to this in the charismatic movement today, I must confess that I personally have seen an overemphasis on "being carried away" interpreted as evidence of spiritual reality. Kathryn Kuhlman, a dear Christian lady, seems to contribute to this with her "slaying in the Spirit." When she points to a person in her meetings, that person is immediately thrown on the floor by some invisible force and is "slain" (faints). Miss Kuhlman, and particularly her followers, seem to think that this is an impressive demonstration of spiritual power. Although she is no doubt a sincere Christian, this kind of impressive display has no part in the New Testament record. In fact, it is paralleled all over the Word as a common occult phenomenon![1] But the ecstasy of the experience is mistaken for the presence of the Holy Spirit. It is probably psychological.

Overemphasis on tongues speaking

This seems to be the whole point of 1 Corinthians 12:4-6.

> There are different kinds of spiritual gifts, but the same Spirit. There are different kinds of service, but the same Lord. There are different kinds of working, but the same God works all of them in all men.

Note Paul's repetition of the word "different." The Corinthians seem to be overly preoccupied

---

[1] Tim Timmons, *Chains of the Spirit* (Washington, D.C.: Canon Press, 1973), p. 27.

with *one* particular manifestation of the Spirit, tongues. Paul wants to stress the variety of the Spirit's working. It is obvious that in twentieth-century charismatic assemblies there is also a tendency to violate this pattern.

Doctrinal error

Paul was faced with some opponents in Corinth who claimed to be uniquely of Christ (1 Cor. 1:12) and who counted his personal presence and lack of miraculous emphasis as an indication that he was not "spiritual" and authoritative (2 Cor. 13:3; 11:21-23; 12:1-4; 10:5-7). These false teachers were totally caught up in the external and the mystical. They were giving the Corinthians a false impression of what really constituted spirituality. They minimized the body, the natural, and the human in the interest of what was considered the spiritual, the supernatural, and the divine. This tendency reveals the beginnings of gnosticism. It is what was behind the denial by these false teachers of the *flesh* in 1 Corinthians 15. They emphasized the resurrection of the *spirit* and denied the bodily resurrection of believers. Thus a preoccupation with spiritual signs and experiences led them to the point of denying the authoritative teaching of Paul.

This, too, has been observed in the contemporary Pentecostal movement. Lest anyone think that this is only hypothetical, it should be pointed out that the third largest Pentecostal movement in America today is a non-Christian unitarian cult. It is called the *United Pentecostal Church,* and is said to have 175,000 members.[2] This is the so-called "oneness" church: it denies that there are three persons in the Trinity, only the second

2 Anthony A. Hoekema, *What About Tongue-Speaking?* (Grand Rapids: Eerdmans, 1966), p. 28.

person exists. This is why they sometimes term themselves the "Jesus Only" movement.

Also, on college campuses another non-Christian cult has arisen, the so-called Way Biblical Research Society, headed up by V. P. Wierwill. This group of Pentecostals denies that Jesus is God, and that the Holy Spirit exists as a separate and distinct member of the Godhead, co-equal with the Father and the Son. This is another brand of the old heresy of unitarianism.

Both of these groups speak in tongues and both are non-Christian. The emphasis on experience and sign gifts has paved the way for these doctrinal aberrations. The false teachings of the Antichrist will find fertile soil in which to take root when they are sown in an atmosphere of theology based on experience.

Emphasis upon signs and revelations as evidence of spiritual reality (2 Cor. 10-13)

The second Corinthian epistle is devoted largely to Paul's defense against the false teachers in Corinth who said that Paul lacked the evidences of power which the false teachers were associating with the spiritual life.

> I now repeat it while absent: On my return I will not spare those who sinned earlier or any of the others, since you are demanding proof that Christ is speaking through me (2 Cor. 13:2, 3).

Paul's authority was in question. They said,

> His letters are weighty and forceful, but in person he is unimpressive and his speaking amounts to nothing (2 Cor. 10:10).

How could Paul be truly so full of the Spirit and yet so personally unimpressive? Paul accuses them of looking only upon surface things.

> You are looking only on the surface of things (2 Cor. 10:7).

The false teachers contrasted their wonderful

new "spiritual" experiences with Paul's poverty. The question was raised, "Haven't we received a fuller Gospel than what Paul preached?" Paul insists there is no other Gospel than the faith alone Gospel that he preached at the first. These teachers were falling into the Galatian and the Colossian error discussed earlier.

Finally, Paul was forced to defend himself by appealing to the fact that he had indeed experienced dreams and revelations. For Paul, these things were secondary and he didn't even like to discuss them. But since it was his supposed lack of them that caused his opponents to assume he was unspiritual, he begins to describe an experience he had in which he actually was taken up into the presence of the Lord.

> Although there is nothing to be gained, I will go on to visions and revelations from the Lord (2 Cor. 12:1).

He now explains an experience and shifts persons, grammatically. He refers to himself as "a man" because he wants to play down the importance of the event as a criterion of true spirituality.

> I know a man in Christ, who fourteen years ago was caught up to the third heaven. Whether it was in the body or out of the body I do not know — God knows. . . . He heard inexpressible things, things that man is not permitted to tell. I will boast about a man like that, but I will not boast about myself, except about my weaknesses (2 Cor. 12:2-5).

This is all he tells of his spiritual experience. There is no elaboration. What a stark contrast to many recitals of spiritual experiences today. I personally have sat by while a person in the charismatic movement described in long and ecstatic detail every aspect of some spiritual experience for a long period of time. Paul's opponents claimed to have experiences of being taken out of their bodies. Recently, I talked to a lady after a charismatic meeting who went on and on about how this happened to her. This was her "conversion experience." Note Paul refused to describe a single thing he saw.

Now note this important change. The false teachers had been asserting that impressive spiritual experiences like tongues, revelations, etc., were evidences of spiritual strength. Paul says he will boast in his "weaknesses," where the false teachers in Corinth boasted in their spiritual experiences which Paul played down as unimportant and surface.

> To keep me from becoming conceited because of these surpassingly great revelations, there was given me a thorn in my flesh, a messenger of Satan, to torment me (2 Cor. 12:7).

A vast amount of spiritual experiences such as those known to the apostle Paul could produce pride. God prevented this in Paul by giving him some sort of "thorn." That had a humbling effect. Paul asked the Lord to remove it three times.

> But he said to me, "My grace is sufficient for you, for my power is made perfect in weakness. Therefore, I will boast all the more gladly about my weaknesses, so that Christ's power may rest on me" (2 Cor. 12:9).

Note, Paul boasted in his weakness *so that* Christ's power would rest upon him. The Corinthians boasted in spiritual experiences as proof that they had power and Paul boasted in weaknesses in order that he might obtain power. Pride is the key hindrance to the experience of power!

> That is why, for Christ's sake, I delight in weaknesses, in insults, in hardships, in persecutions, in difficulties. For when I am weak, then I am strong (2 Cor. 12:10).

Paul says that when he is weak he is strong. The charismatic tongue speakers at Corinth said when you have had revelations and spiritual evidences you are strong! How refreshing to see the apostle boasting in his weaknesses and not describing his experiences of power as contemporary members of the tongues movement are so prone to do. Paul delighted in the very things which the Corinthian false teachers said were evidence of his lack of spiritual power.

THE RESULTS TODAY

There are at least six harmful consequences of the tongues movement that cause one to raise serious question about its claim to be of God.

Living by experience rather than the Word

The unbiblical emphasis on a post-salvation experience of the Holy Spirit has led many believers to begin to live their lives on the basis of feelings rather than faith in the clear promises of Scripture. Their relationship with God and inner happiness depends on a few moments with God conversing with Him in their "tongue." A subtle and gradual movement is traceable in the lives of many from living according to the Scripture to living according to emotion. In the lives of many a personal experience becomes a substitute for clear leading from Scripture or for serious Bible study.

A number of years ago this tendency was illustrated to me vividly in the life of a dear lady in the Northeast. I was in the process at the time of raising some funds for my personal financial needs as a missionary. This lady expressed interest and invited me to come see her. It was an hour and a half drive but I hoped the Lord could give me a ministry in her life. From the moment I walked in the door she never asked me about my work, but apparently had wanted me to come down so she could tell me about the baptism of the Spirit. We talked for several hours. Finally, after listening politely for a long time, I began to share some passages of Scripture with her to evaluate whether or not her tongues experience was really what the New Testament talked about. We discussed the ten criteria of valid New Testament tongues speaking and then I asked her to compare her experience with the Word on each point. To her amazement, there wasn't one point of similarity except the tongue itself. I asked her to seriously evaluate her experience after I left, by going back through the Scriptures and making up her own mind. Four hours later I drove back home. Several days passed and I received a phone call. She told me on the phone how much she appreciated our discussion but the Lord had showed her that she didn't need to study the Bible to find out if her gift was from God. She said right after I left she turned and walked toward the refrigerator of her house. Halfway there she had some kind of experience and the Lord told her that her gift was truly from Him and that she now had peace. Thus, the desire to believe she was experiencing something supernatural was so strong that she avoided subjecting her experience to the test of Scripture for fear that it might prove invalid. She lived her life on feelings. My four hours with her revealed a woman struggling with depression because of a husband who greatly resented her mystical spiritual experiences.

Division among the churches

While directing a student ministry I became aware of the terrible divisions that seem to follow in the wake of the tongues movement. I saw three outstanding evangelistic outreaches for Christ completely destroyed after the charismatic influence began to penetrate among the students. While it is certainly true that in many cases these kinds of splits are just as much the fault of the non-Pentecostal and his unchristian attitudes as

188

it is of the Pentecostal, nevertheless it has been a divisive influence. I find the Pentecostal argument that the splits are a result of Satan's fear of the power that is about to be unleashed unconvincing. It appears to me that the division is based upon the doctrinal aberrations discussed in this book. I tend to see the movement as being used of Satan to purposefully cause division.

Poor testimony to those who do not know Christ

Middle-class America and even most of the youth culture is offended by the emotional excesses of the charismatic movement. In the minds of the average non-Christian, Pentecostalism is identified with the most fanatical form of religious ignorance. In their mind the movement tends to associate Christ with all kinds of violent jerking, convulsions, ecstatic gibberish, and other emotional excesses. While it is true that there are many sincere Christians on the fringes of the movement who have not gone to these emotional excesses, many of those involved in the movement have been involved in them.

A fostering of pride

The ability to speak with tongues is seen in many circles as an achievement and when it has happened the Christian is rather proud of himself.

It is a purely heathen concept

Tongues speaking as manifested today is a purely heathen concept. Never since the Fall has God employed such a method to enable man to communicate with Him. It is entirely unnecessary. Pagan tribes all over the world have been speaking in tongues for centuries. The similarities between their practice and that of the tongues movement are striking. At its root the movement is simply a merger of Christianity with paganism. As demonstrated earlier in this book, the practice of the

189

Corinthians paralleled their involvement in the Greek mystery religions prior to becoming Christians. The same battle that Paul fought in Corinth is being raised again.

It leads to superstition

When I was a new Christian I met a man I'll call Bill. Bill was given to seeing visions and regularly claimed he received direct revelation from God. He saw the Lord working in every conceivable circumstance of life. Every inner impression was examined as to the Lord's leading. One night he called me at midnight because he had a message from the Lord that he had to share with me. Bill was in his forties and lived alone about an hour's drive from my house, but he still wanted to come and deliver the message in person. I was touched by his concern but told him it would be all right with me if it waited till tomorrow. He insisted, so I invited him over. When he arrived he was visibly shaken. At the time I had just decided to go to seminary. Bill was very upset about this ("The letter kills," he said, "but the spirit gives life"), and now he had a message from the Lord warning me not to take this step. He had been reading in Isaiah and the Lord gave him a special revelation that said, "If you go to seminary, your wife will be eaten by lions and you will lose your eternal salvation!" It was rather frightening but I didn't buy it. He lived in a world of superstition which his theology of tongues had fostered. The centrality of the Word had been lost in his life. The last I heard of Bill he was in jail because the "Lord had told him" that he was to disobey constituted authority and not comply with a zoning ordinance!

In conclusion may I reiterate my love for the many people within the tongues movement who have meant much to my life. My objections are doctrinal and not personal. The question is "What saith the Scripture?" In this book we have raised seven crucial questions. I have given answers that are based upon what I think the Bible teaches. Others, equally committed to the final authority of the Word of God within the charismatic movement, have sincere convictions that this is not what the Bible teaches. We must all settle these issues ourselves before the Lord and not simply rely upon human authority, mine or anyone else's. I hope that among the readers of this book there are many "Bereans." It was said of them that they were

> ...of more noble character than the Thessalonians, for they received the message with great eagerness and examined the Scriptures every day to see if what Paul said was true (Acts 17:11).